OOMPH!

PRESS

presents

CONTEMPORARY WORKS IN TRANSLATION

a multilingual anthology

VOL II

OOMPH! Press

© 2018 Published under First Serial Rights.
Original publishers, authors, & translators retain full copyright.

Portions of *Lettere alla Reinserzione Culturale del Disoccupato* (Italic
Pequod, 2013) by Andrea Inglese (trans. by Sara Elena Rossetti)
are reprinted here with permission of Patrician Press.

"Soleil arachnide," from *Soleil arachnide* (Editions Gallimard, 2009) by
Mohammed Khaïr-Eddine, is reprinted here with the permission
of Editions Gallimard, Paris.

Book Layout & Cover Design by Laura Theobald
Logo by Travis Broyles
Curated & Edited by Daniel Beauregard & Alex Gregor

For a complete listing of titles please visit www.oomphpress.com.

CONTEMPORARY WORKS IN TRANSLATION

a multilingual anthology

VOL II

CONTENTS

A LETTER FROM THE EDITORS   VII

A NOTE ON TRANSLATION   IX

ACKNOWLEDGEMENTS   XI

JAIME PINOS (TRANS. BY CARLOS SOTO ROMÁN)   1

GIORGIA ROMAGNOLI (TRANS. BY GIORGIA ROMAGNOLI)   9

MOHAMMED KHAÏR-EDDINE (TRANS. BY JAKE SYERSAK)   13

MARCO GIOVENALE (TRANS. BY DIANA THOW)   25

ALESSANDRO DE FRANCESCO (TRANS. BY ANDREAS BURCKHARDT)   33

NURIT KASZTELAN (TRANS. BY FRANCESCA CRICELLI)   37

FLORINDA FUSCO (TRANS. BY JEAN-LUC DEFROMONT)   41

MARTÍN ARMADA (TRANS. BY SHIRA RUBENSTEIN)   49

DIEGO ALFARO PALMA (TRANS. BY LUCIAN MATTISON)   53

LILIANA MORENO MUÑOZ (TRANS. BY EMILY PASKEVICS)   59

ALESSANDRA GRECO (TRANS. BY MARCELLA GRECO)   65

CLAUDIO BERTONI (TRANS. BY CARLOS SOTO ROMÁN)   71

MARIA GRAZIA CALANDRONE (TRANS. BY JOHANNA BISHOP)   75

MARINA YUSZCZUK (TRANS. BY ALEXIS ALMEIDA)   83

GIANCARLO HUAPAYA (TRANS. BY ILANA LUNA)   87

ANDREA INGLESE (TRANS. BY SARA ELENA ROSSETTI)   95

A LETTER FROM THE EDITORS

We are ecstatic to publish our second volume of *OOMPH! Contemporary Works in Translation: A Multilingual Anthology*. This year's collection showcases work translated from Italian, French, and Spanish, with authors from Italy, Switzerland, Chile, Argentina, Peru, Colombia, Canada, Morocco, and the United States. This year's submissions arrived from Belgium, Switzerland, France, Italy, the United States, and Germany, among other countries in the Americas and Europe. Although our linguistic scope may be slight compared to *Volume I*, we believe what this volume lacks in breadth has been gained in depth.

In these pages you will find works of poetry and short prose appearing in their original language and in English. Since our beginning, we have been committed to publishing every piece that we select in a bilingual, side-by-side format, so that the reader can engage with the translation as much as possible. With the original on the left and the translation on the right, one can simply "cross the gutter" to compare the words in their native language to those presented by the translator. This, we believe, for many reasons, is crucial to developing a deeper understanding of an author and their work; for no language exists in a vacuum, and no translation can be either objectively or completely accurate, either in its form or its meaning. A multilingual approach, then, provides readers with the opportunity to follow the movement between languages and cultures, similar to the processes used by the translators themselves. It is this implicit potential for exchange, which lies in engaging with languages and cultures other than one's own, that embodies the OOMPH! mission and philosophy of translation, detailed in the following section.

It is with great pleasure that we present to you *OOMPH! Contemporary Works in Translation: A Multilingual Anthology Vol II*. As you make your way through its pages, we encourage you to treat the space that separates the work from its translation as a river dividing a city in two, a mountain range partitioning a country into regions, an ocean lying between continents—and forge that river, cross those mountains, and sail across the waters, to hear the voices on the other side.

Thank you for supporting small press publishing and literature in translation.

Alex Gregor & Daniel Beauregard
Founding Editors

A NOTE ON TRANSLATION

Setting down one's thoughts on translation is no simple task. Like the translations themselves, our thoughts about the topic are constantly being shaped and informed by context: our knowledge of a translator and their work, or a particular author; by cultural implications, like the decision to choose a popular author to translate over a less visible one who may have a greater need for recognition; there's also the problem of a "living text," such as when a work is translated and published, then at a later date edited or changed. Judging a translation based on its "accuracy," or the supposed merits of a literal translation seems highly inadequate for this day and age. There's also the difficulty of classifying projects where friends or colleagues are translating each others' work as part of a larger collaboration, such as the case of a work translated from Swedish to Spanish, and later to English.

One of the most appealing aspects of translation is that it is an art much like writing itself. Not everyone is up to the task of mastering another language and teasing out the subtleties and multiple meanings often found in a piece of work, of absorbing a text then choosing the words, turns of phrase, or explanations that will most accurately reflect the writer's intent. In *Illuminations: Essays and Reflections*, philosopher Walter Benjamin equated the art of translation to reanimating when he said, "It is the task of the translator to release in his own language that pure language that is under the spell of another, to liberate the language imprisoned in a work in his re-creation of that work." But what if the translator is working with a living author, or an evolving text? The meaning of translation becomes much deeper and more complex than simply "breathing new life" into an old piece of art, updating for the present day, or fashioning an "accurate" representation. Translation, as we see it, is about the global, present exchange of ideas and art between authors and readers.

It is also prudent to note the different approaches translators use in their processes: while everything from online dictionaries to ancient texts can be useful in translating a work, it's become incredibly easy to research the connotations of words, explore their cultural contexts at different points throughout history, and trace their origins. But this doesn't mean that someone can simply pump a text through a translation engine and expect what comes out to retain much of the beauty and subtlety of the original. Anyone who's spent any time abroad can tell you that some words and phrases—even certain concepts—simply don't exist in other languages. It is the duty of the translator to resolve these issues, whether by hitting upon a close approximation, explaining the problem in a footnote, or inventing some variation on the sort of language used in the original text.

One thing we are certain of, however, is the vital need for translation today, whatever its guiding principles. Anything that can close the gap between cultures, and bring a new audience to voices that have been otherwise ignored, whether due to the prejudices of academia, or other social or economic reasons—often, all three are included in the problem of a notable author in one language gaining recognition in another—will bring us closer in the search for understanding and meaning. When, wherever you are, you are likely facing a number of serious socio-political, economic, and racial issues, translation, and reading translated works, can be a form of resistance. In many ways, translation is a social responsibility, as well as a wonderful and fascinating art. It's our honor to add a drop in the bucket, by printing translations of the most interesting authors outside of the United States that we have come across. We hope, at the very least, we can inspire others to do the same.

ACKNOWLEDGEMENTS

Last year's collection was dedicated to the authors of the original texts and to the translators. This year, we would like to shift the focus away from the work on the page to the communities from which these pieces have sprung. As a publisher that works across languages and cultures, we feel an obligation to acknowledge the people and the places in the foreground of these texts; and as readers, we encourage you to look beyond the texts as well, and even beyond the translators and the authors. For without acknowledging the greater cultural context of the art with which we engage, we run the risk of missing an important piece of the bigger picture—or sometimes the bigger picture itself.

Of course, we would like to express our most sincere gratitude to the authors and translators as well. Without your vision, we would not have the opportunity to gaze into the worlds found in the following pages. In many cases, our translators worked directly with the authors to ensure that the translation be as faithful as possible; all of the contributors went on to play an integral role in the editorial process to ensure that the final manuscript was ready for print. We are eternally grateful for their collaboration.

Additionally, we could not publish this year's journal without showing our appreciation for our dear friend and book designer, Laura Theobald, whose expertise and experience has always allowed us to manifest our vision and ensure that the work is presented in an aesthetically pleasing and reader-friendly format.

Finally, to you, the reader: thank you for investing in the hard work that translators are doing in the world today. Without further ado, we invite you to venture forward into the pages that await.

JAIME PINOS

Jaime Pinos (1970) is a poet, writer, publisher, and producer. He studied sociology and has a degree in Literature and Linguistics from the University of Chile. He has published the following books: *Los Bigotes de Mustafá* (novel, 1997), *Criminal* (poetry, 2003), *Almanaque* (poetry, 2007), *80 días* (multimedia, 2014), and *Vision Periférica* (essay, 2015). He was previously a member of the Lanzallamas Collective, and is one of the founding members of the independent press house, La Calabaza del Diablo.

CARLOS SOTO ROMÁN

Carlos Soto Román (Valparaiso, 1977) is a pharmacist, poet, and translator. He holds a Master of Bioethics from the University of Pennsylvania. He has published the following works in Chile and the United States: *La Marcha de los Quiltros* (1999), *Haikú Minero* (2007), *Cambio y Fuera* (2009), *Philadelphia's Notebooks* (Otoliths, 2011), *Chile Project: [Re-Classified]* (Gauss PDF, 2013), *The Exit Strategy* (Belladonna, 2014), and *Alternative Set of Procedures* (Corollary Press, 2014). As a translator, he has published *Do or DIY: Autoedición, Apropiación, Recontextualización y Plagio* (Das Kapital, 2013), *Bart* by Ron Silliman (Cuadro de Tiza, 2014), *coffee coffee* by Aram Saroyan (Libros del Pez Espiral, 2015), *Patriotismo* by Ryan Eckes (Libros del Pez Espiral, 2015), and *Por favor, no más poesía* by Derek Beaulieu (Libros del Pez Espiral, 2017). His work can be found in the following websites, magazines and journals: *Octopus, Otoliths, Fox Chase Review, Flying Fish, Revista Laboratorio, eL Paper, Caesura, Dear Navigator, Apiary, Eleven Eleven, Poetic Labor Project Blog, Where Eagles Dare,* PEN *American Center Blog, Gaceta de Estudios Latinoamericanos, Los Desconocidos de Siempre, Capitalism Nature Socialism, P-Queue, Summer Stock, Revista Grifo, COYDUP, Newport Review, Crux Desperationis, Letras en Línea, Hinchas de Poesía, Clock, The American Poetry Review, Mandorla, Jacket2,* and *Aufgabe*. He is a MacDowell Fellow and recipient of grants from the Chilean Council for Culture and the Arts for Creation and Translation projects. He also was the curator of the cooperative anthology of U.S. poetry *Elective Affinities*.

NOTA AL MARGEN

La poesía como
TRABAJO DE CAMPO

El poema como
ESTADO DE COSAS

El poeta como
NARRADOR OBSERVADOR

LA VOLUNTAD ES EL ARMA

Trabajar
Trabajar
Cerrar la boca y trabajar

La voluntad es el arma.

Sobre la poesía como vanidad
sobre la poesía como depredación
la voluntad de lucha
prevalecerá

Los verdaderos enemigos de la poesía chilena
los verdaderamente importantes
están fuera de la poesía chilena

Al embajador norteamericano, a las Buenas Familias
a los altos funcionarios, a los dueños
les importa un bledo la poesía chilena
no saben que existe la poesía chilena

La poesía chilena es un boliche de esquina
un bazar de barrio pobre

Intemperie

Una carpa de circo en medio del desierto
un desierto largo y angosto a orillas del Pacífico
un largo y angosto pasillo sin salida aparente

No hay Poder en la poesía chilena
Pequeñas ventajas, prebendas menores

SIDE NOTE

Poetry as
FIELD WORK

The poem as
STATE OF AFFAIRS

The poet as
OBSERVER NARRATOR

THE WILL IS THE WEAPON

To work
To work
To keep your mouth shut and work

The will is the weapon.

The will to fight
shall prevail
over poetry as vanity
over poetry as predation

The real enemies of Chilean poetry
the ones that really matter
are outside Chilean poetry

The U.S. Ambassador, the Good Families
the senior officials, the landowners
they don't give a damn about Chilean poetry
they don't know that Chilean poetry exists

Chilean Poetry is a corner dive bar
a thrift store in the ghetto

Being out in the open

A circus tent in the middle of the desert
a long narrow desert on the Pacific coast
a long narrow passage with no apparent exit

There is no Power in Chilean poetry
Small advantages, minor perks

algo de dinero, poco
muy poco

Tristísimo espectáculo
la carrera de perros
por llegar a ser
Poeta Único/Poeta Nacional

Cachacascán en la pista
frente a las gradas vacías.

La poesía como comprensión
La poesía como exigencia
La poesía como generosidad
La poesía como valentía
La poesía como honestidad

Con uno mismo y con los otros
En la vida propia y en la vida de los otros

Esa voluntad de lucha
día a día
palabra a palabra
tarde o temprano
prevalecerá

Escribir
Leer

Aprender a leer
aprender a leer bien

Trabajar
Trabajar
Cerrar la boca y trabajar

Hacer poesía
en medio del desierto
en la inmensidad de la arena
hacer un fuego
mantenerlo encendido
en medio del frío y la ventolera

Comprender lo que dice la ola
cuando martilla en la playa
una y otra vez

some money, a little
very little

A tremendously sad spectacle
the dog race
to become
the Only Poet / the National Poet

A wrestling match on the track
in front of the empty stands.

Poetry as understanding
Poetry as a requirement
Poetry as generosity
Poetry as courage
Poetry as honesty

With oneself and with others
In your own life and in the lives of others

That will to fight
day by day
word by word
sooner or later
will prevail

To write
To read

To learn to read
to learn to read well

To work
To work
To keep your mouth shut and work

To make poetry
in the middle of the desert
in the vastness of the sand
to make a fire
to keep it burning
in the middle of the cold and the gale

To understand what the wave says
when it hammers on the beach
over and over again

EL PAÍS SE QUEMA

El país se quema.
Los peores incendios forestales de la década.
Decenas de miles de hectáreas.
Arden bosques milenarios bajo el cielo inmenso de la Patagonia.
Arden grandes extensiones artificiales de pinos y eucaliptos en Bío Bío.
Un cerco de fuego baja desde los cerros y amenaza las ciudades de la costa central.

Los incendios son intencionales.
¿Quién quemó, quién quema este país?
El gobierno acusa a las comunidades mapuche de iniciar el fuego en Bío Bío.
Pero el fuego se inició hace mucho tiempo allí.
El fuego cruzado entre las comunidades y el capital forestal.
Las forestales arrasan los cultivos, talan las especies nativas.
Plantan en su lugar grandes extensiones artificiales de pinos y eucaliptos.
El pino radiata crece allí casi el doble que en otras partes del mundo.
Eso es mucha madera. Eso es mucho dinero.
El pino radiata exuda una resina que se inflama a los 35 grados.
El fuego consume primero las copas de los árboles.
Avanza desde arriba hacia abajo. Cae como una tormenta
sobre las extensiones artificiales de árboles idénticos como postes de teléfono.

El mudo corazón del bosque devorado por las llamas,
el estruendo de los árboles al caer
bajo la tormenta de fuego.

El país se quema.
¿Quién quemó, quién quema este país?
¿Cuándo se inició el incendio?
El fuego se inició hace mucho tiempo aquí.
Tal vez con la bandera chilena hecha una flama
durante el bombardeo a La Moneda.
Tal vez con la quema de libros en las calles
durante el estado de sitio.
Tal vez con Sebastián Acevedo como una antorcha
en la plaza de Concepción.
Tal vez con Rojas Denegri como una antorcha
frente a la patrulla militar que lo detuvo.
Tal vez con Eduardo Miño como una antorcha
frente al Palacio de Gobierno.
Los árboles y las personas se queman
hace mucho tiempo en este país.

Vivir en un país en llamas,
en un país que se quema.
Vivir a orillas de un largo y angosto río de fuego.
Vivir en el corazón del bosque,
aguantar el desplome. La tormenta.

THE COUNTRY IS BURNING

The country is burning.
The worst forest fires of the decade.
Thousands of acres.
Millenary forests burning up under the immense sky of the Patagonia.
Large artificial extensions of pines & eucalyptus burning up in Bio Bio.
A wall of fire coming down the hills threatening the cities of the central coast.

Fires are intentional.
Who burned, who's burning this country?
The government accuses Mapuche communities of starting the fire in Bio Bio.
But the fire started long time ago there.
The crossfire between communities and forest capital.
The lumber industry devastates crops, cut down native species.
Planting instead large artificial extensions of pines & eucalyptus.
Radiata pine grows there twice as much as in other parts of the world.
That's a lot of wood. That's a lot of money.
Radiata pine exudes a resin that ignites at 95 degrees F.
Fire consumes the treetops first.
It moves from top to bottom. Falling like a storm
over the artificial extensions of trees that look like utility poles.

The mute heart of the forest devoured by the flames,
the roar of the trees falling
under the firestorm.

The country is burning.
Who burned, who's burning this country?
When did the fire start?
The fire started long time ago here.
Maybe with the Chilean flag turned into a flame
during the bombing of La Moneda.
Maybe during the burning of books on the streets
during the state of siege.
Maybe with Sebastian Acevedo as a torch
in the square of Concepcion.
Maybe with Rojas Denegri like a torch
in front of the military patrol that detained him.
Maybe with Eduardo Miño as a torch
in front of the Government Palace.
Trees and people have been burning
for a long time in this country.

To live in a country in flames,
in a burning country.
To live on the banks of a long and narrow river of fire.
To live in the heart of the forest.
to endure the collapse. The storm.

GIORGIA ROMAGNOLI

Giorgia Romagnoli is a young Italian poet, translator, and student of literature currently living in Macerata, Italy. Since 2012, she has participated in the blog eexxiitt.blogspot.it. You can find many of her texts online, including her ebook, *Prove tecniche di trasmissione*. She has translated Dmitrij Prigov and Ciaran Carson, among others. She's also the editor of *Porà*, an online magazine of writing and translation.

ARIANNA

*3)

Il gioco dell'oca, snakes and ladders; i bambini non sanno di imbrogliare. Guardandolo dall'alto si aboliscono tutte le sue regole; se Teseo avesse avuto una mappa avrebbe compiuto la sua missione molto più velocemente e il filo non sarebbe stato necessario. Dedalo. Minotauro. Neanche Canova è riuscito a rappresentare tutta la sua – impotenza. Arianna. Saggia o folle. Tornare indietro dopo aver esplorato ogni nuovo corridoio o non ripercorrere due volte la stessa via nello stesso senso a meno che non si sia costretti a farlo. Il filo non sarebbe necessario. Dedalo. Le ali di cera. Una degna sepoltura. Una statua senza cera. Unicursale, ad albero, a rizoma. Non lo sapevano; per loro era solo irrisolvibile.

Snakes and ladders. Aleatorietà determinante. Il segnaposto che si ferma ai piedi di una scala sale; quello che si ferma sulla bocca di un serpente scivola.

*4)

Anche l'orecchio interno ha una forma simile, eppure il suono non ci si perde. Sa esattamente quale strada seguire. Gira in tondo attraverso scale e svolte obbligate.
Contiene l'organo dell'equilibrio che va educato sin da piccoli per riuscire a stare in piedi, camminare, andare in bicicletta, ecc.

Capita però che un trauma o un grande spavento facciano sì che il suono si perda (/disperda, che perda la via), che l'impulso sia errato o mal interpretato, che il liquido vibri dal verso sbagliato o che ci sia un'ostruzione.

L'aggettivo russo глухой [gluchój] può assumere i significati di:

1. sordo (anche fig.)
2. remoto, solitario
3. chiuso
4. cieco
5. molto aderente
6. folto
7. disabitato, senza vita

Come se non si potesse vivere, senza quella vibrazione.

ARIADNE

*3)

The game of the goose, snakes and ladders; children don't know they are cheating. Watching it from high, all rules are abolished; with a map, Theseus would have completed his mission more quickly and he wouldn't have needed the thread. Daedalus. Minotaur. Even Canova could not represent all his – helplessness. Ariadne. Wise or foolish. Coming back after the exploration of each new hallway or not walking twice the same path in the same direction, unless you are obliged to. Daedalus. Wings of wax. A worthy burial. A statue without wax. Unicursal, tree-shape, rhizomatic. They didn't know; for them it was only unsolvable.

Snakes and ladders. It's the randomness that determines. The game piece that stops at the bottom of a ladder goes up; the one that stops on the mouth of a snake slides.

*4)

The internal ear also has a similar shape, but the sound doesn't get lost in it. It knows exactly the right way. It goes round and round through ladders and obliged turns.
It contains the organ of equilibrium that needs to be educated starting from childhood in order to be able to stand, walk, ride a bicycle, etc.

But sometimes it happens that a trauma or a big fear makes the sound lose its way (/scatter, get lost); the impulse could be mistaken or misunderstood, the liquid could vibrate in the wrong direction, or there could be an obstruction.

The Russian adjective глухой [gluchój] can mean:

1. deaf (also fig.)
2. remote, lonely
3. close
4. blind
5. very close-fitting
6. bushy
7. uninhabited, without life

As if you couldn't live without that tremble.

MOHAMMED KHAÏR-EDDINE

Mohammed Khaïr-Eddine was born in 1941 in Tafraout, Morocco. Widely regarded as one of the most influential avant garde intellectuals and writers of the Maghreb region of northern Africa, he is especially renowned for his "guerilla linguistic" literary style, which critically engages the cultural milieu of postcolonial Moroccan society. In 1965, he was exiled to France for his radical political views. After spending some time in Paris, he eventually returned to Morocco in 1979 and died in Rabat, the capital, in 1995.

JAKE SYERSAK

Jake Syersak received his MFA from the University of Arizona and is currently a PhD student in English and Creative Writing at the University of Georgia. He is the author of *Yield Architecture* (forthcoming, Burnside Books, 2018) and several chapbooks. His poems have appeared in *Black Warrior Review, Colorado Review, Verse Daily, Omniverse*, and elsewhere. He edits *Cloud Rodeo,* serves as a contributing editor for Letter Machine Editions, and co-curates the Yumfactory Reading Series in Athens, GA.

SOLEIL ARACHNIDE

soleil contus des éprouvettes
entre l'hiéroglyphe simple des arachnides

les mouchent regardent
mon occiput où le soleil tassé en fèces
fait un sinistre avec la terre crieuse de nos dépouilles
vieux faussaire
je décrasse un poète tombé dans ses rétines
un poète qui ne dit pas aux lunes
son nom comblé de fosses jalouses d'astres
et qui inventorie les dents vertes du dégel
myriade buccin sextant protoplasme résine
où l'oeil sacrifie la légende intentée
aux carcasses mal cadenassées des myriapodes
prudemment par les geôles bées des rancunes
les rengaines inextirpées dictent mon élan
bicyclette trappe coeur jeté tel vieux bloc
d'anciennetés à sac et de futurs rentrés
dans les grimaces du froid donneur des mots-cavernes

les pèse-mémoires ont fendu comme élytre
l'aciérie fauteuse
de rejetons d'oiseaux hennissant pour un cistre
d'ors frappés du simulacre d'ailes
où gigote l'absence inouïe des involucres

frénésie faste éclipses alcool
avec cette tranchée qui ne répond
des guerres données par ma mémoire
oubliée des saints rompus tel hages bigles
sur ce ciel chu
parmi moi seul où la tribu jette ses vermines

Midi, la ville. Factions, sarbacanes, philtres. Les enfants jettent des fûts sur les carrioles. Affaire tirée au clair. L'Arme m'entend. Je suis assis sur un amas de journaux et de rêves mal commentés. Je grouille: pentatomes. Ni printemps, ni été. Sommeils et oiseaux morts, atteints d'un songe inacceptable. Je fume kif et ciel. Les stalactites en auront pour l'éternité. Derrière moi, un trône à démettre.

ARACHNID SUN

the sun's contusion of test subjects
enters the simple hieroglyph of arachnids

the flies gaze
into my occipital lobe where the sun gels into feces
generating what's ominous in the earthly screams of our remains
old forger
I'm polishing up a fallen poet from those retinas
a poet who doesn't speak to moons
whose name fills with the jealous pits of stars
& who takes inventory of the green teeth after a thaw
myriad buccine sextant protoplasm resin
of an eye sacrifices the legend on trial
to the poorly locked-up carcasses of myriapods
prudently dumbstruck through the penitentiaries by spite
my impulses are dictated by inexplicable refrains
bicycle trapdoor disposable heart this old block
of looted antiquities & irretrievable futures
in the grimaces of the frigid yielder of cavernous vocabulary

these weigh-ins of memory have split like wings of elytra
faulty steelworks
of fledglings' whinnying after some golden
zither struck by the simulacra of wings
where the unacknowledged absence of crown whorls wriggle

frenzy splendor eclipses liquor
with its trench that's unresponsive
to any wars yielded by my memory
rendered oblivious by prostrate saints what short-sighted hags
on this plummeted sky
partly my lonesome self into which the tribe dumps its vermin

Noon, in town. Guards, blowpipes, potions. The children sling barrels onto carts. Business as usual. This weapon understands me. I'm seated on a heap of newsprint & badly annotated dreams. I teem: stink bugs. Neither spring, nor summer. Sleepiness & dying birds, infected by some intolerable delusion. I smoke dope & sky. The stalactites will possess that for all eternity. Behind me, a throne to fuck up.

Pertuis de mer. Grande ou petite. Pélamide. Au marché, même statues. Le coiffeur érige un koutoubia dans cette rue fichée avant l'Ordre. Ses cheveux m'ont colporté. Plus rien. J'enquête. L'étoile va son triple fil: torturée. Comment a-t-on pu la chanter? Rouge-verte! Cent dictons l'assument.

L'Afrique est un véritable uniforme. Grilles. Je te dégomme. Lumière à contre-joie. Affres et gloire. Dans le cœur vide de l'épine, la contiguïté acclame mon oeil. Ce sont les silences, les grandes syncopes. On cloue des polyptères sur mon échine mieux arrosée qu'un visage de prophète. De mes paumes gicle l'aube. Tiens, non, je retire ma face de graisse noircie.

un roi seul ictère une crypte
flingue aumône lynch faux dollar
je décrypte la nuit franche des inédits du sable
fornique lacère ma fugue et erre sur l'orgasme
des vins âpres d'un temps sans boussole où l'index
du bédouin pile toute monnaie et sans rancune
fourbit un astre à meme ton ombre qui s'abîme
quand je porte ton cadavre au sommier horoscopique
des cailloux de l'enquête cousue avec mon rire

J'assiste au étripements: GENNEVILLIERS. D'un verre cannelé sort un diable biffe le nuage proxénétique ourdi par ma casse. Je vous causes des transes. Vous seriez vanne dans ma rupture.

                                        ILS ANNONCENT
                                        MA MORT

cette affiche court l'air sondé
crève
mais crève qui n'enfante
qu'un roi soldé
ni noir et dont la croupe lève les stries gammées
sur l'enfance marchant dans le blanc cruel de ta cornée

il habite une bauge luxuriante entre des tessons d'astres des tonnerres précoces des cloportes et des fausses entreprises dont la prière noue la dictée catégorique aux créneaux d'ambre et de caroubes par quoi s'infirme le soleil que je broie lorsque j'ai soif sous les médailles les obus reçus les sacs de farine et les pains de sucre qui sont mon sexe unique—je m'accoude aux attentats mais je m'emporte trope vite sachant les courses à faire aux combles des ruines pas anciennes dans l'Aube authentique gonflée d'un remugle inhalatoire telle la chevelure-feu de la fille née de mon désespoir rouge pustule et tantôt bleue Elle roule sur mon dos son ossement et s'envole pas très haut mais assez loin puisque je la cherche et la vois tout juste bleu rouge jamais blanche plutôt verte se roulant sur ses coiffes retenant péniblement ses étincelles pour mieux m'oblitérer.

Outlet to the sea. Large or small. Skipjack tuna. At the market, the same statues. The hairdresser pitches a koutoubia through the street before The Order. His hair was the selling point. Nothing else. I should investigate. The star goes about its three-ply: tortured. How could you possibly set that to music? Red-green! One hundred proverbs assume it's so.

Africa really is a uniform. Prison bars. I'm going to peel you away. Light against the joy-grain. Pangs & glory. In the empty-hearted spine, contiguity cheers my eye onward. These are the silences, the long blackouts. These reedfish screwed into my spine are better irrigated than a prophet's face. Dawn squirts out of my palms. Well, nah, I'm just peeling blackened grease off my face.

a lonely king jaundices a crypt
shoots down amity lynch faux dollar
I decrypt the candid night from the unseen sand
that fuck-lacerates my fugue rollicking with the orgasm
of wines after an era without compass wherein the index
of this bedouin stacks cash & without spite
sparkles up a star in your very shadow engulfing itself
when I lug your corpse to the horoscopic pedestal
from the pebbles of inquiry sewn together with my laugh.

I aid the disemboweling: GENNEVILLIERS. Out of a fluted glass comes a devil who strikes the flesh-peddling cloud woven from my fragments. I entrance you. You'll serve as valve to my rupture.

THEY'RE BROADCASTING
MY DEATH

this ad does its rounds on the air
feverishly
but feverishly nurturing
not any african
but a paid-off king
whose ass raises swastikas
over the infancy goose-stepping its way into your cruel white cornea

He dwells in a luxurious pigsty laden with the shards of the stars' premature thunder of dummy enterprises & louses whose prayer knots easily distinguishable dictation to slots of amber & carob sinking the sun I crush in my thirst under the medals the spent artillery shells the sacks of sweetbreads & flour that orient my unique sex—I lean into the attacks but I get carried away too fast with my knowledge of what errands need run amongst the attics ruins not so ancient inside authentic Dawn swollen with the arid lungful of hair flaring from the lady my reddish despair gave birth to pimple & soon to be blue She rolls her bones across my backside & flies not too high but just far enough since I'm searching for & see it just red blue never white rather green rolling along its headdresses laboriously retaining the scintillation all the better to obliterate me with.

Au bout de la ville l'extase de mes indifférences SOLEIL ET TRUITE traqués dans un bassin qui m'avait litté-
ralement aimé je me suis effondré dans un rire sommaire sous les branchettes sans autre oiseau que ma fatigue
c'étaient le chant la rapide querelle du trépas sonnant la mer pas loin hélée en trombe avant que l'eau n'ait
remanié mon identité GRAND BÛCHER POUR HOMME TOUT SEUL et qui s'appelle éclipse langue
morte JOUR TUÉ PRIS AU SERIEUX depuis grand-père et son ancêtre sous la menace d'un accident sur-
venu on ne saurait jamais comment Fumisterie belle pour éviter les crosses comme autant de sonorités volées
aux jalons qui me multiplient moi boui-boui Sacquée la saveur Nous avons colmaté le nombril trop vu avec
une poignée de ciel sinistré forcé les coffres où vous cachiez l'œil malheureux du printemps. Il vous attirait vous
attristait de loin lorsqu'à coté et même en moi se levait votre silence fuligineux dans une masse de buildings
d'usines et de masures qui narguent le pécule taillé dans vos langues qui sont nos plus graves rixes.

nopal-terre-galet-terre
et si mon anus fait une ruade
où la germination excellent du songe
tire ses tarots
mon élan fronde et cible oui mon éclat
d'ordre réprimé et de travail
scrute tes affaires dans les Raffaeolo fastes
et les Bismarck d'où ton naufrage me décoche
l'étoile assise dans ma rotule.

L'enfance inclinée me stranglera. Pure ! Toilette de céraste. Le sable donnait sa voix au petit jour.

SOLEIL
haridelle mais je compte le trajet
entre les flamants noirs et le journal
des steppes soulevées en razzias de polices
dans la fausse incantation des latérites

j'ai l'œil à tordre les inscriptions où tu m'assois plus que mer étalée sur tes subterfuges de yacht et d'ivoire désert ni roide ni jaune les vrais alytes disent mes scindements mes oubliettes sans quoi la mort serait un carcan je
me casse dans cet œil m'y couche et te remplace par un afflux de sangs précipités fais-moi vacciner donne-moi
la pluie qui ne tombera pas.

la terre goulue les sagaies jeunes de ta flibuste
les nuits de spasmes et de sarcasmes
et les jours de gifles allongées mieux que ciel
donneur mais acquitte-moi des mascarades
dont mon aile porte la limite
où s'annule la péripétie de ce prophète
ni sur l'if oublié sous mon aisselle

On the outskirts of town the ecstasy of my indifferences SUN & TROUT hunted through a pond that had literally loved me I dismantled into perfunctory laughter under the twiglettes without the other bird my fatigue it was the singing the rapid quarrel of death ringing out the not too far off sea taking off before the water had redesigned my identity GREAT PYRE RESERVED FOR MAN & calls itself eclipse the dead tongue SNUFFED-OUT DAY TAKEN SERIOUSLY since grandpa & his ancestor under the reign of a surfaced wreck we wouldn't ever know how The illusionist made handsome for his evasion of the crosiers like so many acoustics stolen from their milestones multiplying me Dive bar of low appeal We've clogged the too visible naval with a handful of utter sky unhinged the vaults where you stowed the miserable eye of spring. It addressed you distressed you from afar when from the side & even from inside me arose your sooty silence from a mess of factories & hovels that ridicule the nest-egg in your tongues wherein resides our most serious fight.

prickly pear-earth-buoy-earth
& my anus if it bucks
where the excellent germination of illusion
shuffles its tarot
it's my impulse to draw back & take aim yes my luster
of suppressed order & toil
messes up your business in splendors of Raffaello
& Bismarcks where your sinking reveals me
the star dwelling in my patella.

The slope of youth will strangle me. Utterly! A lavatory of vipers. The sand yielded its voice to daybreak.

SUN
Nag nag nag yet I account for the trajectory
between black flamingos & newsprint
steps escalating into police raids
in the false incantation of laterites

I have the eye to wring out inscriptions from where you seat me more than sea spread all over your subterfuges of yachts & desert ivory neither rigid nor yellow the true alytidae may say dividing my obscurities without death would be a straightjacket I burst into this eye puts me to bed & swaps you for an influx of precipitating blood go ahead make me vaccinate give me the rain that won't fall

the earth chokes down the young assegais of your piracy
nights of sarcasms & spasms
& days of slaps in the face stretched longer than sky
preacher come now forgive me these masquerades
my wing lugs the border of
where this prophet's peripeteia cancels itself out
not over the yew tree under my armpit

ni sur l'eau
du mastoc forniquant avec un sexe coupé
par les jardiniers qui portent ma nuit

il me fit la chasse mais je m'en tirais toujours je pouvais voler ne pas voter l'Urne s'ouvrait dans le soleil comme un poulpe ravi de ce que la mer fût retournée pour tenter les acrobaties préméditées et saigner son furoncle à ce ramassis d'hommes dont la particularité est de s'appeler peuple bâton cravate journal charrette ou balle perdue nous ne visitions ni minaret ni grenier nous avions d'autres yeux des mains étudiées subrepticement à l'ombre des iotas conçus par les belles fourmis du désespoir riant soir et matin jusqu'au nuage le plus aigri et qui n'a pas encore salué le chergui des voix salvatrices. J'avais jeté mon cartable dans une ornière La ville s'était enfoncée Son électrisme sonnait comme des pièces de monnaie rendues sur un comptoir de cuivre

j'étais l'œuf le boa la torture
du gris-gris démembré sur mon écorce
le temps accouplé aux mots faiseurs de rouille
pour trônes jouant
avec mes billes et mes prunelles
mon nez plus loin tel une grimace jugée à la légère Il me consommait me déboîtait les chevilles les marronnes élites de mes querelles et je le traitais dans une farine de blé noir et le livrais non pas aux vaches mais aux poussins frileux de mon sang qu'il osait colmater de bouse d'alucites et de gravier je ne sais combien de fois contemplé par les somptueux poètes refoulés à la frontière du gouffre je démolissais les temples brûlais les archives du monde et mettais l'Homme Négatif en marche On le voyait passer comme un cerceau flamboyant entre les barbes nouvellement taillées les costumes de la saison et les affaires publiques On le disait fée faillite ange paniqué mais on se trompait puisque j'avais fermé tous les musées les mosquées les églises et les industries où le Mot n'avait plus cours mais dès que je revoyais un pré un oiseau un arbre fleuri ou pas j'appelais l'hiver et l'engageais immédiatement à parfaire le terrain de sorte que je pouvais sculpter une maison blanche sur la page noire du temps et promener quiètement les rires sauvages que j'arrachais aux hommes mi-songes mi-crosses par l'allée fondamentale où vous m'avez égaré dès l'école et même après m'avoir décousu

Hirsute. Vache bileuse. Salades. Articulations, mais ce sexe fébrile dérape vers la ceinture des villes moisies. Non, Madame la Crevette. Vertèbre et sel. C'est l'assiette. Elle va beaucoup mieux ce matin. Carats pour un soir de risée géniale. Verts tel quel. Les petits potins. Les vieux marsouins. Les lacertes vaccinés par mon ouïe. Voyeur, tu me confères une vertu marsupialisante. Il vient d'astres bien polis. Moi, le Jus Parfumé ? Tu flingues pas ça. File ton vin frelaté que je dicte à la ronde. Il s'en va tant j'avais mal aux panses et puis on n'en discute plus jamais. Le vieux corbeau qu'a pris ses dents au croco pauvre croco. Il fait le soldat de la culture male piochée. Pas arrosée par nos soleils. Pas brillamment en tout cas. je ne vous connais pas plus que mon anus à part que je vous ai entrevu les grisailles de mes ébouriffements. Il repart comme pas une. DANS CE VIEUX BORDEL DES LETTRES MAUDITES ET REMAUDITES QUE FICHE D'UN TEMPS DE PETITES ÉLITES QUI S'ENFORMENT SUR LE LAURIER ROSE DEVENU JAUNE À FORCE ? Il revient deux jours plus tard, Je veux des têtes d'épingles, Je veux tes crottes sédatives. Pas de crottes, pas de sacre ! Je vais te saper bonhomme, t'auras qu'à te laisser prendre les mesures. je tourne le dogme, j'vais l'épine. Baffe, demis sans hiver, la mousse, ça m'enracine parfaitement. Mais j'aime pas les hauts plats, les bides où mon caca et celui du vrai bon dieu circulent avec aisance. je vais toutes les dix minutes aux chiottes. Je ne me détaille pas dans le trou. Je

nor over the water
of fornicating heaps with sex cut
by the landscapers who wear my night

He's hunting me but I'm nearly out of here I could fly not to vote the Ballot Box opened in the sun like an ecstatic octopus of what the sea had thrown back in an attempt of premeditated acrobatics & drain its boil into this clusterfuck of man whose peculiarity it is to call itself the people baton tie newspaper wheelbarrow or stray bullet we looked closely into neither minaret nor breadbasket we had eyes aside from those hands studied discretely in the shadows of iotas perceived by beautiful ants of anguish laughing evening & morning up to the most curdled cloud & who to this day still haven't saluted the chergui wind of salvational voices. I'd tossed my knapsack into a ditch The town quelled itself The electrolysis of it rang like loose coins rendering the copper of a countertop

I was the egg the boa the torture
of the gris-gris dismembered across my exterior
time coupled with the words artisans of rust
for thrones toying
with my marbles & my pupils
my nose longer than a grimace to put it lightly It used me up it lashed me by my ankles the elite fugitive slaves of my querulousness & I dredged it in black wheat flour & abandoned it not to the steers but the timorous young chicks of my blood it dared to clog full of gravel & mealworm dung dwelled upon I've no idea how many times by those sumptuous poets pushed back from the brink of the abyss I demolished the temples set fire to the archives of the world & set The Negative Man in motion You could see him like a flamboyant hoop between the beards freshly styled seasonal fashion & public affairs It was said to be a faerie panicked bankrupt angel but they were wrong because I had shut down all the museums the mosques the churches & industries where The Word had run its course but as soon as I looked again a meadow a bird a tree in bloom or not I called out for winter & entreated him immediately to perfect the ground so that I might sculpt a white cottage on the black page of weather & tip-toe quietly around the wild laughter that I wrestled from man mid-illusion mid-crosier by the fundamental alley where ever since school you disoriented me & right after having rendered me apart

Disheveled. Worry wart. Word-salad. Articulations, yet this restless sex drifts toward the belt of moldy cities. No, Miss Prawn. Vertebra & salt. That's the dish. She feels much better this morning. Carats for the brilliant laughing stock of night. Greens as it is. Short gossips. The old porpoises. Lacertae vaccinated by my hearing. Peeping tom, you impart me with a marsupial virtue. He comes from well-polished stars. Me, the perfumed juice? Don't shoot that. Follow your contaminated wine that I'm dictating to no one in particular. He goes away so often that it's tied my stomach in knots no one discusses it anymore. That old crow buried its teeth in the croc poor croc. He makes a poor likeness of the soldier of culture. Unbasted by our suns. Unbrilliantly in any case. I don't know you any better than my anus other than I caught a glimpse of you between the gray scale of my dishevelment. It departs again as no other did. WITHIN THIS OLD BORDELLO OF DAMNED & DAMNED AGAIN LETTERS WHO GIVES A DAMN ABOUT A TIME WHEN THE TINIEST OF ELITES SUFFERING ON THEIR LAURELS WENT YELLOW BY FORCE? It came back two days later, I want those pinheads, I want those sedatory shits. No shits, no coronation! I'm gonna bring you down, man, you'd better take precautions. I'm souring dogma, I'm thorning this place up. Shocker, halves without winter, without froth: that roots me in place perfectly. But I don't care for fancy cuisine, the potbellies where my caca & whatever's true of gracious

pratique, savez-vous comment…l'AFFRE dont personne n'a jamais osé dire un mot. C'est vilain, tais-toi. Non j'peux plus. Je ne bouffe pas votre astuce. Voici mes denrées, mais rythmes rares et intrépides, tout à fait bas ; mes canevas de fourches plus grimaçantes que grimacées : ouvertes comme gueule de chiot qu'a jamais fait ses canines. On me donne pas cet os, Monsieur Le Fringué. On m'évite qua j'ai hurlé…Ou bien fiche ça dans le trou et discute pas.

Conasses ces petites directeurs de feuilles d'algues indigestes ! T'es d'accord sang-paul-miche qui ronges en même temps que moi les involucres farcis d'étoiles des faux drapeaux ? L'enquête énorme à dégotter.
le CALUMET n'est pas de ma fabrication
je fais des laisses pour promener les vrais soleils
j'électre et ne promets pas
un soir une vide saison un cil ça ne fait rien
tout hurle pour être dit
répété commis commetant
avec les sacres noirs du désert qui rapplique
à tout moment

Le drapeau n'est plus buvable ! La légende est odieuse ! Nous somme les Nouveau Morts !

cette roseraie où la nuit me perturbe s'accommode mal da ma soif
sauts d'onces vacheries gâchées
dents pas gâtées mais ébréchées par les vins aigres
le soir
quand j'applique à mon front le nu des grottes fouillées
un buvard me sèche me hante
me fait goûter le sel des mots
à ne dire
à presque personne sinon à ceux qui trempent
dans le sang pur soldé d'un soleil rhacophore

god circulate with ease. Every 10 minutes I'm on the toilet. I won't spell myself out in the hole. I'm practicing, would you like to know how...TORMENTS of which no one would dare mention. That's naughty, shut up. No I can't anymore. I won't swallow your cheap tricks. My only nourishment is those rare & intrepid rhythms, undeniably low. My canvas of forks more contorting than contorted. Open as a puppy's maw that never fanged. No one throws me a bone, Mr. Fancypants. We try not to scream...Or else plug that hole & forget it altogether.

Little director fuckwits made of indigestible algae! You actually agree with that bloody-Richie-Rich boob, the one who's chewing the involucral rosettes stuffed full of falsely-starred flags? What an enormous question to unearth.
CALUMET is not my handiwork
I make leashes to walk authentic suns
I electra & promise nothing
a night an empty season an eyelash it does nothing
everything screams to be said
repeated perpetrated perpetually
by the sacred blacks of desert that in each moment
reapply

The flag is no longer palatable! Its legend is odious! We are those Newly Deceased!

This rosary where night badly perturbs me accommodates my thirst
leaps of snow leopards nasty waste
teeth unspoiled nevertheless blemished by the bitter wines
this evening
while I apply the nudity of the excavated caves to my forehead
blotting paper will dry me out will haunt me
will force me to taste the words' salt
to not tell
nearly anyone except those who soak
in the pure blood indebted to a rhacophorous sun

MARCO GIOVENALE

Marco Giovenale (1969) lives in Rome, where he works as an editor and translator. He's a contributor to *alfabeta2* and *l'immaginazione*, as well as the founder and editor of gammm.org (2006). In 2011, he took part in the Bury Text Festival in Manchester. His work has appeared in the following magazines: *il verri*, *l'immaginazione*, *Nuovi Argomenti*, *Action Poétique*, *Nioques*, *OEI*, *Aufgabe*, and *Capitalism Nature Socialism*. His recently published books in Italian include: *Strettoie* (Arcipelago Itaca, 2017), *Il paziente crede di essere* (Gorilla Sapiens, 2016), *Maniera nera* (Aragno, 2015), *Delvaux* (Oèdipus, 2013), *In rebus* (Zona, 2012), *Shelter* (Donzelli, 2010), and *La casa esposta* (Le Lettere, 2007). He has also published the following books in English: *a gunless tea* (Dusie, 2007), *CDK* (Tir-aux-pigeons, 2009), *anachromisms* (Ahsahta Press, 2014), and *white while* (Gauss PDF, 2014). His work in "asemic writing" has been published in the following books: *Sibille asemantiche* (La camera verde, 2008) and *Asemic Sibyls* (Red Fox Press, 2013). Follow him online at slowforward.net.

DIANA THOW

Diana Thow's translations of Italian poetry include Amelia Rosselli's *Hospital Series* (Otis Press/Seismicity Books, 2017) and *Impromptu* (Guernica Editions, 2014). Her translation, with Sarah Stickney, of Elisa Biagini's *The Guest in the Wood* (Chelsea Editions, 2013) won the Best Translated Book Award in 2014. She holds an MFA in literary translation from the University of Iowa, and is currently a doctoral candidate in Comparative Literature at the University of California, Berkeley.

frasi in ordine alla descrizione del cuoco
che vanno bene anche per un'altra professione (ma solo per una)

dice che ci sarà una rivoluzione dal basso

da due settimane

cammina dondolando leggermente

apre la porta e poi la richiude per mantenere l'aria fresca dentro

stacca la fattura 2-2-(8)

non ama le strutture pubbliche, gli ospedali faranno parte del quadro della rivoluzione

gli è venuta questa idea

un toner parla di sé in prima persona

il pappagallo si strofina sulla palla da tennis

affettuosamente (è un modo di dire)

ha comprato un nuovo disco rigido

ha gli occhi marroni

la sua fidanzata è belga ma non è ancora tornata dal belgio

da due settimane

domenica va in barca, è un momento di relax

inutile telefonare

gli è venuta questa idea

a series of phrases for describing the cook
that also apply to another profession (but only one)

he says there will be a revolution from below

in two weeks

he walks, swaying lightly

opens the door and then closes it again to keep the air inside cool

detaches the bill 2-2-(8)

doesn't love public structures, hospitals will take part in the revolutionary plan

this idea came to him

a toner speaks about itself in the first person

the parrot rubs itself against the tennis ball

affectionately (it's a figure of speech)

he bought a new hard disk

he has brown eyes

his girlfriend is Belgian but hasn't come back from Belgium

in two weeks

Sunday he's boating, a moment to relax

it's useless to call

this idea came to him

senza titolo

un elicottero abbastanza sicuro.
anche la rete della pellicola, meglio se dentro, è sicura.
il museo è sicuro, e la settimana.
sono sicuri i ricavati, è sicuro il tiraggio.
l'autunno, di solito, anche se ci sono delle variazioni, è sicuro.
i locali notturni sono sicuri.
il respingimento, il battito dei gatti, anche:
sicuri.
l'immaginazione è sicura.
l'ascolto è sicuro.
la linea è sicura.
c'è un posto sicuro.
il monitoraggio dell'area è sicuro.
i materiali sono sicuri, se ne siamo sicuri.
l'iban è sicuro perché serve solo per ricevere soldi.
è sicuro il lunedì, anche il martedì, si direbbe.
è sicuro l'inizio, in sostanza è sicura la fine.
la religione sotterranea è piuttosto sicura, e quella aerea.
la pratica è sicura.
il mouse è sicuro.
gli impiegati sono sicuri.
sono sicure le proporzioni.
la sicura è sicura, lo dice il nome.
lo stroboscopio pure, lui è sicuro.
con l'oscilloscopio.
il fumo è sicuro.
è sicuro il calcestruzzo.
come sono sicuri i punti cardinali, il sud.
la baia è sicura.
la polizia è sicura sempre.
la lucentezza è sicura.
la notte anche vedi che è sicura.
il compressore è sicuro.
il ladro è sicuro, siamo sicuri.
per le stesse ragioni è sicuro il gioco.
il cavo è sicuro.
la musica è sicura.

untitled

a rather safe helicopter
and the web of film, better if inside, is safe.
the museum is safe, and the week.
the proceeds are safe, the draft is safe.
autumn, normally, even if there are variations, is safe.
the night clubs are safe.
the repulsion, the beating of cats, also:
safe.
the imagination is safe.
listening is safe.
the line is safe.
there is a safe place.
monitoring of the area is safe.
the materials are safe, if we're safe.
the iban is safe because it's only needed to receive money.
Monday is safe, Tuesday too, it seems.
the beginning is safe, and on the whole the end is too.
the underground religion is very safe, and the aerial one.
the praxis is safe.
the mouse is safe.
the employees are safe.
the proportions are safe.
the safe is safe, as the name suggests.
the stroboscope, too, is safe.
with the oscilloscope.
the smoke is safe.
the concrete is safe.
as the cardinal points are safe, the south.
the bay is safe.
the police are always safe.
the luster is safe.
see, the night too is safe.
the compressor is safe.
the thief is safe, we are safe.
the game is safe for the same reasons.
the cable is safe.
the music is safe.

filmabilità

la cosa più importante per gli asserragliati è raggiungere le loro costanti antropologiche (il bar, le automobili):
ci sono i miei figli qui fuori che mi aspettano.

essere una ballerina di talento, l'amministratore in fuga, la stagnina del motel gay, il prete fissato con le lucertole:
questa è la roncola che uso.

aspettare fino all'ultimo prima di far saltare col gas la baracca di legno al margine del bosco:
ci nascondiamo nei barili d'acciaio della birra.

all'avvicinarsi, mancare il bersaglio, soccombere alle rane, dato che i soccorsi sono tenuti alla larga dalla tempesta
e la lavatrice che faceva andare la dinamo della radio per la lampadina ha finito il ciclo: shit, the sheriff's gone.

filmability

the most important thing for those barricaded is to reach their anthropological constants (the bar, the cars): my children are here outside they are waiting for me.

to be a talented dancer, the fleeing administrator, the gay motel's plumber, the priest obsessed with lizards: this is the pruning hook I use.

to wait until the last moment before blowing the wooden shack at the edge of the forest up with gas: we hide in steel vats of beer.

at the approach, missing the mark, succumb to the frogs, given that aid is kept at bay due to the storm and the washing machine that set off the light bulb dynamo of the radio completed its cycle: *shit, the sheriff's gone.*

ALESSANDRO DE FRANCESCO

Alessandro De Francesco (Italy, 1981) is a poet, artist and essayist living in Basel and Brussels. Since 2008, Alessandro has been a visiting professor at the European Graduate School and an artist-in-residence at the International BeHave Program Luxembourg, the STEIM Amsterdam, and the Kunsthalle Mulhouse. He taught poetry and creative writing at the École Normale Supérieure in Paris and was an artistic research fellow at the Research Centre for Visual Poetics at the University of Antwerp. He has read, performed, and exhibited work at the Kelly Writers House at U-Penn, CUNY, the Fondation Louis Vuitton, the Centre Pompidou, the MAMCS in Strasbourg, the Berlin University of the Arts, and elsewhere. Alessandro holds a PhD in Poetics from the University of Paris-Sorbonne. His recent books include *Continuum: Writings on Poetry as Artistic Practice* (The Hague: Uitgeverij, 2015), *La Vision à distance* (Paris: MIX., 2015), and *Remote Vision: Poetry 1999-2015* (New York: Punctum Books, 2016). Follow him online at www.alessandrodefrancesco.net

ANDREAS BURKHARDT

Andreas Burckhardt
(born in Locarno, Switzerland, 1986) is the author of *A Sanctuary of Sounds* (punctum, 2013).

nel tardo pomeriggio di ritorno dal lavoro si rende conto
che una massa corporea molto alta sta immobile nell'arco
della porta tra una stanza e l'altra   sembra che lo osservi ma
non ha né arti né occhi né forma definita   non dice niente
non vuole niente   è un territorio di tessuti

spesso volumi convessi appesantiscono i rami degli alberi
talora sono fatti di foglie che ritmano l'aria   altre volte da
condensazioni bianche dove scavano gallerie   i
rami allora tracciano volte   passaggi di sotto   cunei lunghi

dentro i volumi   nelle intercapedini scavate dai vettori
o nella tana vuota ricoperta di foglie vengono forse
posizionati obiettivi che abbracciano un ampio arco di
paesaggio   cercando informazione

tempo minerale   corpo vitreo   tegumenti
e più tardi   o allo stesso tempo   27 immigrati rumeni chiusi
dentro una camionetta vengono   scoperti sul territorio e
rinviati oltre il confine

in una teca del british museum un uomo sumero in bronzo
sta aspettando   davanti a sé   da 4000 anni   con occhi
lisci e senza pupille   esplora spazi siderali   il rumore
della membrana   la bacca rossa che cade nel ruscello mentre
nessuno passa

late afternoon   coming home from work   he realizes
that a highly dense body stands motionless in the door's arch
between rooms   it seems to be observing him but it
doesn't have eyes nor a definite shape   it doesn't say anything
doesn't want anything   it's a territory of tissues

often   convex   volumes   weigh   down   the   tree's
branches   at   times   they   are   made   of   leaves
giving rhythm to the air   at other times of white
condensations excavating galleries   the branches then
trace vaults   passages below   elongated wedges

inside the volumes   in   the   interstices   excavated
by vectors or in the empty den covered by leaves
perhaps lenses are positioned embracing a wide range
of landscape   searching   for   information

mineral time   vitreous body   teguments
and later   or at the same time   27 Romanian immigrants
closed inside a small truck are discovered on the territory and
sent back across the border

in a display case at the British Museum a bronze Sumerian
man is waiting   in front of him   for 4000 years with
smooth eyes without pupils explores sidereal spaces the noise
of the membrane   the red berry that falls in the stream
while no one passes

NURIT KASZTELAN

Nurit Kasztelan (Buenos Aires,1982) has published *Movimientos Incorpóreos*, *Teoremas* (Uruguay) and *Lógica de los accidentes* (Argentina and Spain). She also writes drama and has directed some of her small plays. She performed at the poetry reading series *La manzana en el gusano* and used to coedit the magazine *No-retornable*, where she published translations of Alda Merini and Louise Glück. Now she runs the publisher Excursiones and has a bookstore at her house. She has participated in many poetry festivals and has been translated into Portuguese.

FRANCESCA CRICELLI

Francesca Cricelli (Ribeirão Preto, 1982) has published *Repátria* (Selo Demônio Negro, 2015, Brazil), *Tudo que toca o olhar* (Casa Impressora Almería, 2013, Brazil), and *Repátria* (Carta Canta, 2017, Italy). She has also translated Elena Ferrante in Brazil, as well as poets such as Ungaretti, Pasolini, Jacopone da Todi, Luzi, and Rondoni. She is a PhD student at the University of São Paulo (USP), where she works on the love letters of Giuseppe Ungaretti to Bruna Bianca (Un vivente amore di poesie, lettere a Bruna Bianco, Giuseppe Ungaretti, Mondadori). She has traveled to many countries to read her poems, including Spain, Italy, USA, Nicaragua, Turkey, India, and China.

UNA RED INVISIBLE

Hay una red invisible de gente
que sostiene las cosas
que hace algo para que vos
no te caigas
te quedes en tus cinco años.
Estás afuera en el jardín
con tu frasco de vidrio
atrapando las hormigas
las juntás con las manos
con cuidado de que no se mueran
que se acomoden de forma precisa
en la hoja que para vos es un colchón.
Todavía entendés
solo la mitad de las cosas del mundo
y la que ahora quiere el frasco de vidrio
soy yo
para apresar este pequeño momento
donde el presente
está más allá de vos y de mí.

AN INVISIBLE NET

There's an invisible net of people
that holds things together
that does something for you
not to fall
to keep you in your five years.
You are out in the garden
with your glass bottle
catching ants
you hold them in your hand
careful enough so they don't die
so they can take a well defined place
on a leaf that is to you a mattress.
You still understand
only half of the things in the world
and who now wants the glass bottle
is me
to trap these tiny moments
where the present
is beyond you and me.

FLORINDA FUSCO

Florinda Fusco's work has appeared in several Italian journals including *il verri, poetiche, Nuovi Argomenti, Filologia critica, Allegoria,* and *Testo a fronte,* as well as the following foreign publications: *Aufgabe* (New York), *The New Revue of Literature* (Los Angeles), *La Nouvelle Revue Francaise* (Paris), *Action Poétique* (Paris), *Exit* (Montréal), and *Le Sigle XX* (Paris). Her poetry has been included in anthologies of Italian poetry, such as *Akusma: Forme della poesia contemporanea* (Metauro 2000), *Sololimoni* (Shake 20001), *Verso, l'immagine: Sulla soglia tra arte e poesia* (Fondazione Baruchello), *Parola Plurale* (Sossella 2006), *Nuovi poeti italiani* (Tighler 2006), *La creatività femminile* (Lieto Colle 2006), and *Fuori dal cielo* (Empiria, 2007), etc. Her books of poetry include *linee* (Editrice Zona 2001) and *Il libro delle madonne scure* (Mazzoli 2003), which won the National Delfini Prize for poetry in 2003, as well as *Tre Opere* (Oedipus Ed. 2009) and *Thérèse* (Polimata Ed. 2011). Her texts have been translated into English, French, and Spanish.

JEAN-LUC DEFROMONT

Jean-Luc Defromont is a translator currently living in Berlin. He has been a French language Lecturer at the University of Bari, as well as an English teacher at a French school.

LA SIGNORA CON L'ERMELLINO

0.1

al trasloco

apri i cassetti e raccogli tutte le posate

svuota l'anta destra e la sinistra del thé e dello zucchero rimasti

togli la consolle, il tavolo e le sedie attorno prendi la poltrona

smonta l'armadio e raccogli tutti i vestiti anche quello lungo rosa

col cappello a fiori togli il libro, il peso, il dolore, la siringa

smonta la camera da letto e poi il salotto dalla parete

prendi lo specchio e tutte le figure impresse nel suo fondo sposta

lo scaffale togli il lume, il comò, l'acqua di colonia

e il centrino di merletto svuota il cesto pieno di piccoli oggetti mai veduti

smonta la stanza dei morti e quella dei vivi svuota i mobili

svuotali uno ad uno, ogni tazza ogni piattino svuota la memoria

rappresa al fondo della tazza svuota la cucina, il frigo che congelava

congela il corpo, il taglio

THE LADY WITH AN ERMINE

0.1

to your moving out

open the drawers   and gather all the cutlery

behind the right door   and the left one   take out the remaining tea and sugar

remove the console, the table   and the chairs around it   take the armchair

dismantle the dresser   and gather all the clothes   even the long pink dress

with the flowered hat   remove the book, the weight, the pain, the syringe

dismantle the bedroom   and then the drawing room   off the wall

take the mirror   and all the figures stamped on its bottom   push aside

the bookcase   remove the lamp, the chest, the cologne water

and the lace doily   empty the basket   full of small objects never seen

dismantle the room of the dead and that of the living   empty the cupboards

empty them one by one, every cup every saucer   empty the memory

clotted at the bottom of the cup   empty the kitchen, the fridge that freezed

freeze the body, the cut

0.2

non conosco   i raggi ultravioletti   i lati del metallo   l'interno della plastica

non conosco la profondità di un quadrato

metto una donna grassa   al centro di una stanza vuota

ritaglio un piccolo foro nel muro

la donna grassa non conosce il blu

perché non sia sola   riempio la stanza di acqua e pesciolini

inscrivo un quadrato   sulla sua pianta del piede   nel quadrato disegno un piccolo bosco

la figura si eleva   galleggia nell' aria   tra le bollicine

vesto la donna di fuxia   le metto quattro nocelline nella mano

il quadrato è sul pavimento   cancello il bosco   perché la donna non abbia paura

ora la metto al centro della figura

i suoi piedi segnano i secondi

adesso posso arrestare il tempo

I don't know   the ultraviolet rays   the edges of metal   the inside of plastic

I don't know the depth of a square

I put a fat woman   at the center of an empty room

I carve out a small hole in the wall

the fat woman doesn't know blue

I fill the room with water and small fish   so that she won't be alone

I inscribe a square   on her foot sole   in the square I draw a small wood

the figure rises up   floats in the air   between the bubbles

I dress up the woman in fuchsia   I put four small walnuts in her hand

the square is on the floor   I erase the small wood   so that the woman won't be afraid

now I put her at the center of the figure

her feet mark the seconds

now I can stop time

0.3

spingo le dita sul vetro

guardo

oltre il vetro

      io seduta su un trono   come un papa

il vestito rosso scuro   gli anelli   la grande croce d'oro al collo

davanti a me   teste troncate come da ghigliottina

      il cielo si stacca   il volto della terra si squaglia

      insieme al mio trucco

spingo le dita insanguinate
  sul vetro infranto

al di là del vetro

      tutto è identico a se stesso

      le scarpe alle scarpe   i cappelli ai cappelli   le tazze alle tazze

      le linee dei volti
      all'indifferenza del boia

0.3

I press my fingers on the glass

I watch

beyond the glass

      myself sitting on a throne   like a pope

the dark red robe   the rings   the big golden cross at the neck

in front of me   heads severed as if by guillotine

      the sky comes off   the face of the earth melts away

      together with my make-up

I press my bloodstained fingers
    on the smashed glass

beyond the glass

      everything is identical to itself

   shoes to shoes   hair to hair   cups to cups

      the lines of the faces
      to the headsman's indifference

MARTÍN ARMADA

Martín Armada was born in Buenos Aires, Argentina in 1979. He has published the poetry collections *El estero* (Gog & Magog, 2006), *Ahab* (VOX, 2011), and *Hombre sentado ahí* (Determinado Rumor, 2015).

SHIRA RUBENSTEIN

Shira Rubenstein was born in Saratoga Springs, New York and has lived in the United States, Costa Rica, Chile, and Argentina. She received her B.A. in Creative Writing from Brandeis University. Her poems and translations have appeared previously in *OOMPH!*, Window Cat Press, and *The Brooklyn Rail*. She currently lives in Eugene, Oregon.

El silencio es el cuero
que separa lo que es mío
de lo que nunca va a ser mío,
sencillo, claro es el silencio,
las hojas no se mueven
no pasan autos,
no piensan llamar los que se fueron
así empieza el futuro, sin ruido.

Comí carne y soñé que la ciudad ardía,
sobre una terraza mirábamos el agua
de un tanque hervir.
No había pasado ni futuro para odiar,
nuestra vida de pronto comenzó
el trabajo de la ceniza:
oscurecer
los lagos, las piedras, el pasto,
los caballos, las ramas, las hojas,
los pájaros, los árboles, las montañas, el cielo.

El agua cae del vaso que se rompe
y en la luz parece oro.
Podría ser un poema
sobre mi abuela que hoy enterró al último
de sus hermanos varones,
pero no.
El agua cae del vaso que se rompe
y en la luz parece oro.

Soñás con un patio en el que hay una higuera
entre piedras,
con una nube que se lleva un parte del agua,
alguien te dice que hagas las cosas solo.

Soñás con una mesa larga,
caras detrás del humo
que sube de los platos,
cualquiera puede ser padre de cualquiera
cualquiera puede ser hijo de cualquiera.

Silence is the flesh
separating what is mine
from what will never be mine–
silence, clear and simple,
no rustling leaves
no passing cars
no one who moved on thinks to call.
This is how the future begins:
without a sound.

        I ate meat and dreamed the city burned.
        From a terrace we watched water
        boil in a tank.
        There was no past, no future to hate.
        Our life began at once
        the work of ash:
        it darkened
        lake, stone, grass,
        horse, branch, leaf,
        bird, tree, mountain, sky.

Water spills from the breaking glass
and the light turns it golden.
This could be a poem
about my grandmother who today buried
the last of her brothers,
but it is not.
Water spills from the breaking glass
and the light turns it golden.

        You dream of a patio with a fig tree
        among stones,
        a cloud carrying away part of the water,
        someone who tells you to do it by yourself.

        You dream of a long table,
        faces behind the smoke
        rising from the platters.
        Anyone could be anyone's father.
        Anyone could be anyone's son.

DIEGO ALFARO PALMA

Diego Alfaro Palma (Limache, Chile, 1984) is a poet and editor. He is the author of two poetry books: *Paseantes* (2009, Ediciones del Temple) and *Tordo*, winner of the Santiago Literary Prize 2015 (Ediciones del Dock, Argentina, 2016 | Editorial Cuneta, Chile, 2014). He edited *Homage to Ezra Pound* (Universitaria, 2010) and *Collected Poems of Cecilia Casanova* (Universidad de Valparaíso, 2013). His most recent work, *Litoral Central*, was published in Argentina by Audisea and in Chile by Pez Espiral. He is the founder of publisher Limache250 in Buenos Aires, Argentina, where he currently resides.

LUCIAN MATTISON

Argentinean-US poet and translator Lucian Mattison is the author of two books of poetry: *Reaper's Milonga* (YesYes Books, 2018) and *Peregrine Nation* (Dynamo Verlag, 2017). His poetry, short fiction, and translations have appeared in numerous journals including *Four Way Review*, *Hayden's Ferry Review*, *Hobart*, *Muzzle*, *Nano Fiction*, *The Nashville Review*, *The Offing*, *Puerto Del Sol*, and *Waxwing*. He currently lives in DC and edits poetry for Big Lucks. Follow him at Lucianmattison.com

BALLENERO

La primera condición para la caza de ballenas: recibir el
arpón al centro del centro de la desazón; asimilar tu soledad
de calamar gigante. Toda profundidad es solo geografía
inhóspita, porque nada hay sino el hierro en carne,
recortando barbas, aquilatando grasas. La delicadeza se
abandona en este escenario, coreografía de sangre, su tira y
afloja: la cultura de arrancar robles de raíz, gritando al cielo
¡soy un hombre!
Y el terror: el terror va por derecho propio.

CIÉNAGA

El juego entre el marco oscuro de sus gafas y los bigotes
canos daban la impresión de estar frente a un marinero
retirado, sin embargo sólo su dedo índice había recorrido
los meridianos de un mapa amarillento y del que hacía
repasar copias con lápices de cera: cada imperio, cada
océano una tonalidad distinta. Él enseñó las fronteras,
nombres que la humanidad dio a lo que siempre creyó suyo.
Colgaba en la pizarra un pliego arrugado y con palabras
proyectaba una batalla entre griegos y persas, al caballo de
Alejandro avanzando aguerrido sobre la arena del tiempo, las
lanzas de los gladiadores entrando en un costado. Cristo
tomaba en él sentido, la empresa imposible del amor,
mientras en la misa el sacerdote quebrando la ostia, cumplía
con graficarnos la dispersión de los hombres, la separación
de los mares, lo invisible abriéndose paso a través de la materia.
Él se difuminó en el vacío que dejan las cosas, el piano
descansado de sus hijos, la sábana de su mujer estirada, sus
notas resguardadas en un cajón sin cerradura.

WHALER

The first condition for whale hunting: take
a harpoon to the center of chagrin's center; assimilate
your giant squid solitude. All depth is only inhospitable
geography because there is nothing but iron in the flesh,
trimming beards, appraising blubber. Delicacy is
abandoned on this stage, choreography of blood, your ebb and
flow: culture of pulling oaks by the root, shouting at the sky,
I am a man!
And the terror: terror moves by its own will.

SWAMP

The play between the dark mark of his glasses and white mustache
gave the impression of being in front of a retired sailor,
nevertheless, only his index finger had traced
the meridians of a yellowed map of which he made
us retrace with wax pencils: every empire, every
ocean a distinct tonality. He taught the frontiers,
names that humanity gave to that which they always thought theirs.
Hung on the blackboard was a wrinkled sheet of paper and with words
it projected a battle between Greeks and Persians, to Alexander's horse
advancing, war worn over the sands of time,
the gladiators' lances piercing a side. Christ
took in sense, the impossible enterprise of love,
while at the same time the priest, breaking off the rib, fulfilled
his duty of charting the dispersal of man, the parting
of seas, the invisible giving way through matter.
He faded in the void left by things, the piano
given rest from his children, his woman's stretched bed sheet, his
notes put away in a drawer without a lock.

VI

El Buda es toda compasión
Montreal es toda compasión
en Chile la noche es eterna
bajo ella se cierran las flores del loto
el sonido del tren como esporas
el viento curte nuestra piel
la realidad es una pantalla táctil
la sobriedad de sus íconos
el mantra del río nos levanta cada mañana
carpinteros astillan sus manos
la energía fluye hacia las industrias
toda posesión es engaño
tú y yo quisimos tener personas
coleccionar sus gestos y objetos
la conocí por cuatros años sin llegar a nada
llegar a nada Jeanne es un impulso vital
el minimalismo en que nos deja el amor
Bertolt Brecht se sentaba en su cama a escribir
los viejos libros explican la sabiduría:
apartarse de las luchas del mundo
transcurrir sin inquietudes la brevedad del tiempo
librarse de la violencia dar bien por mal
no satisfacer los deseos olvidarlos
y quisiéramos vivir bajo un parrón los domingos
tener una casa en el lago como la de ella
ver veranos enteros el polvo envolver al cardo
los tordos se posan en ellos a trinar
sus autos entran a terrenos privados
el camino se adoquina
sus lanchas descansan en los muelles
una vez se escapó de esos almuerzos
rodeando la orilla hasta mezclarse en un desfile
comió empanadas manchando su vestido
mientras volantines se desplomaban en los sauces
ahora solo me la encuentro en los sueños
duermo poco mucho tal vez casi nada
y he intentado aprender las cartas del tarot para saber si me piensa
y sin embargo debemos anular todo pensamiento
dejar que la voz retumbe hasta la espalda
entrecerrar los ojos repetir palabras sin sentirlas
descubrir el velo hacia el vacío
la ciencia es inútil en esos puntos
es por eso te pido Jeanne olvida Buenos Aires
respira con ritmo regular
no violentes la realidad
sé como las cortinas sacudirse en el lago.

VI

The Buddha is all compassion
Montreal is all compassion
in Chile the night is eternal
lotus flowers close beneath her
the sound of the train like spores
the wind hardens our skin
reality is a touchscreen
the sobriety of its icons
the mantra of the river wakes us every morning
the carpenters spall their hands
energy flows toward industry
all possession is deception
you and I wanted to have personas
collect their gestures and objects
I knew her for four years without getting anywhere
not getting anywhere Jeanne is a vital impulse
the minimalism in which love leaves us
Bertolt Brecht sat on his bed to write
old books explain wisdom:
depart from worldly fights
let elapse without concern the brevity of time
liberate yourself from violence impart good not evil
don't satisfy desires forget them
and we want to live under a grape arbor on Sundays
have a lake house like hers
see whole summers in dust wrap the thistle
the blackbirds perch on them to trill
their cars enter private land
the road turns to cobblestone
their boats relax on the docks
one time she escaped from those lunches
rounding the banks until falling in with a parade
she ate empanadas staining her suit
while kites plummeted into the willows
now I only find her in dreams
I sleep a little a lot maybe almost never
and I tried to learn tarot to see if she thinks of me
and yet we should nullify all thoughts
let the voice resound to the spine
squint eyes and repeat words without understanding them
discover the veil before the void
science is useless at these points
that's why I ask you Jeanne forget Buenos Aires
breathe in a regular rhythm
do not force reality
be as the curtains sway in the lake.

LILIANA MORENO MUÑOZ

Liliana Moreno Muñoz (1974) is a Colombian poet, dancer, and scriptwriter. She holds a BA in Linguistics and Literature from Universidad Distrital Francisco José de Caldas and an MA in Hispanic American Literature from the Instituto Caro y Cuervo in Bogotá. She is the artistic co-director of *Saraswati: Artes Integradas*, as well as the co-creator and manager of the poetry project *Al aire libro*. Her full-length poetry collection, *En lengua de bruja (Partitura para cuerpo y voz)*, was published in 2015, and her poems, stories, and essays have been published in national and international journals and magazines, as well as in poetry anthologies from Colombia and Mexico: *Oscuro es el canto de la lluvia* (1997), *Inventario a contraluz* (2000), *Diez mujeres poetas le cantan a la tierra* (2015) and *Voces de tinta* (2016). She is also a professor in the Literary Creation undergraduate program at the Universidad Central in Bogotá, and the director of literary workshops via IDARTES and the Casa de la Cultura de Chía. She has participated in various individual collective creative projects, including "Poesía en escena," "La Divina con medias" (2013), and the stage poetry production "Tríptico del fervor" (2016). She is currently developing a research project on experimental literary creation called "Scriptures from the Body."

EMILY PASKEVICS

Emily Paskevics is a writer and editor currently based in Montréal, Canada. She is the author of *The Night Was Animal, or: Methods in the Art of Rogue Taxidermy* (Dancing Girl Press, 2014). Her work can also be read in *Hart House Review*, *Vallum Magazine*, *Acta Victoriana*, and *Rogue Agent Journal*, among others. She is a regular contributor to a variety of platforms and publications, including *Lola Who*, *LunaLuna Magazine*, and *Culture Trip*. With special thanks to Andrés Pérez Vásquez for his translation insights and suggestions.

FUGA DEL SENTIDO

Como marioneta a quien le cortan los hilos...
En la espantosa quietud
sólo el brillo del cuchillo que pasó.

AL CANTAR DE LOS PÁJAROS DE SANGRE

Se evapora el color
y se desteje toda piel
a la sombra de mis dedos.

Entre la multitud que se asoma al espejo,
me busco.

No hay reposo en el olvido,
ni se agita el horizonte
al cruzar el huracán de la memoria.

Recién nacida y muerta,
mi voz.

Alguien aquí
y lejos,
un relámpago.

ESCAPING CONSCIOUSNESS

Like a marionette whose strings have been split...
In the ghostlike silence
just the glint of the knife
as it passed.

WITH THE SINGING OF THE BIRDS OF BLOOD

The colour melts
and all of my skin is unstitched
at the shadow of my fingertips.

In the crowds that peer into the mirror,
I seek myself.

There is no rest in oblivion,
nor is the horizon shaken
at the crossing of the hurricane
of memory.

Recently birthed and departed,
my voice.

Someone here
and distant—
the lightning strikes.

... PÁJAROS DE SANGRE

Amanece en mi cuerpo,
Afilados rayos del sol
cruzan las ramas celestes
y trinos caudalosos
brotan de los nidos.

soy el fango que cruzas,
el viento que asciende
tu espalda vegetal,
secreto revés de la piel,
nervadura de hierbabuena.
Tu erizado plumaje de arpía
borra los mundos, los muros.

Se hunden las miradas
en la luminosa caballera del día
como semillas del grito original.

... SANGRE

Las ciudades ya no tienen rostro
todo es piel
y en la piel mil ojos
y en los ojos el olor
        el olor de la música
        como ceniza de flores.

... BIRDS OF BLOOD

It dawns in my body.
Sharp rays of the sun
cross the celestial branches
and a frenzy of birdsong
springs from the nests.

I am the mud that you cross,
the wind that rises and climbs
along your vegetal spine,
this secret underside of the skin,
these dark veins of spearmint.
Harpy-like, your bristling feathers
and clawed wings erase
the worlds, the walls.

The otherworldly glances sink
in the bright, wild strands of the day
like seeds from the birthing cry,
the original scream.

... BLOOD

The cities no longer have faces
everything is skin
and in the skin a thousand eyes
and in the eyes the scent
            the scent of the music
            like the ash of flowers.

ALESSANDRA GRECO

Alessandra Greco was born in Rome in 1969. She lives and works in Florence.

MARCELLA GRECO

Marcella Greco grew up in Rome. She is an interpreter and translator professionally formed at the High School for Interpreters and Translators, in Rome, with specialization at the Stafford House Tutorial College, Canterbury, Marburg University, Frankfurt, and Sprachen Und Dolmetscher Institut, Muenchen. She works as a freelance interpreter in many international conferences, summits, workshops, exhibitions, meetings, events, EU projects, web streaming and press conferences, TV and radio shows, private, corporate and board meetings, interviews, and accompanying delegations and ministers. She has been proud to translate for outstanding politicians and authorities, covering the full range of interpreting events, from big summits to personal meetings. With over 19 years of experience, she provides written translations for private customers, companies, agencies, international organizations, private and public associations, NGOs, authorities, institutions and media in many fields including politics, business and economics, finance, trading, public health and social affairs, education, literature, medicine and research, corporate management, computer science, IT, energy, new technologies and infrastructures, automobile production, food and environment, EU, UN, and institutional affairs. As for the literary sector, she has been editor of the book *Joshua Immanuel The Christ* by Dr. Stylianos Atteshlis (The Stoa Series, 2001), and co-translator of the novel *Our Nig* by Harriet E. Wilson.

(25 decibel è un sussurro)
(scrizione che il cervello sia uno spazio geografico e architetturale)
(giorno#X)

I.

(25 decibel è un sussurro)

le stelle cadono   dell'inchiostro lo stilo meticoloso   cadono sulla pelle come punti vuoti la porta si chiude
come una grande croce   le strutture hanno domini complementari   la stella neve   la neve manifesta tutto in
perfettissimo silenzio   quando è il segno che hai paura di morire   *cosa dicevi? vieni nel mio buio più profondo*
le stelle cadono dentro uno spazio bianco   non c'è alcuna sovrapposizione   cadono in scie fanno un piccolo
lago di lisci ami   a lato la testa l'anello l'universo   gocce acustiche tenute in un'unica perla   parole
discontinue rescissioni secondo settimo primo terzo taglio affondi   però tutti di ammirazione e di
affezione in direzioni invertite e polari   abbacinanti e seduttrici che era buia la notte che tu mi chiedevi
se andava tutto bene in onde ai bordi dei foglietti temporali   preparando oltre l'insidia quelle stelle morenti
e un netto concorso di luci   la chioma scintillante degli alberi in aprile   o come si apre un fiore secondo
consonanze   l'albero genealogico occupa un foglio e le spiegazioni gli altri due senza guardare fa osservare:
le radici continuano a crescere   viste da un'altra angolazione   il naufragio della voce nell'aria   lo smisurato
ingrandire dei suoni nei luoghi chiusi il vetro poroso tempo dentro un cannone   la dimensione degli spazi in
questi astri contenuti quindicesima notomia di un suono all'orecchio

II.

(scrizione che il cervello sia uno spazio geografico e architetturale)

lla piccola sfenoide incisura del rostro lacrimale   the female nude drawing faces & expressions   ove scorrere
diluito ipermnesico medizin und plastik nervo che si fa cristallo sfera sul labbro superiore e al di sopra degli
angoli boccali   diradare   et de la duplicité monstrueuse avec planches coloriées de anditu et olfactu borgo
spinae praeparate cerea campo cutaneo di proiezione di tutti i centri remoti icones oculi humani il punto alla
sera non viene all'esterno ma solo al mattino trascina rariora artifiziale e le sue pareti dilatano e si restringono
matutinus occorre pensare alleanza in astri organorum fabrica autem catoptrum microcosmicum de lactibus
sive lacteis venis microcosmi in laminis aereis et ecce foramen unum in pariet liquido ostendens l'impulso a
correre dei venti pone davanti questa immagine lembi di fondo della ragione un circolo in un più grande
circolo svanire in plain view parola in ordine suffuso in start ci sono lacrime nelle cose fin dove continua corr
in questo modo la sua rapidità diventa normale da uno spazio vuoto nel quale siamo svegli

(25 decibel is a whisper)
(scription that the brain is a geographic and architectural space)
(giorno#X)

I.

(25 decibel is a whisper)

stars fall down   the cautious ink stylus   fall on skin   as void points   the door shuts like a big cross   structures have complementary domains   the snow star   the overt snow   everything in all-perfect silence   when it's the sign that you are afraid of dying   *what did you say? come into my deepest darkness*   stars fall down in a white space   there is no overlapping   fall in trails   forming a small lake of smooth hooks   to the side the head   the ring   the universe   acoustic drops held in a single pearl   discontinuous words   dissections second seventh first third cut stabs   but all of admiration and affection   in reversed and polar directions blinding and seductive   as it was so dark   the night you asked me   if everithing was all right   in waves at the edges of the temporal leaves   preparing beyond the snare   those dying stars   and a bright contest of lights   the sparkling hairy trees   in April   or as a flower opens   according to consonances   the ancestral tree takes up a sheet   and the explainations the other two   without looking it induces to observe: roots continue to grow   viewed from another angle   the shipwreck of the voice in the air   boundless enlargement of sounds in closed places the porous time glass in a gun the scope of spaces contained in these stars   fifteenth notomy of a sound to the ear

II.

(scription that the brain is a geographic and architectural space)

t the small sphinhaul   incision of the lacrimal rostrum   *female nude drawing faces & expressions*   where flowing diluted hypermnesic medizin und plastik nerve turning into crystal   sphere on the upper lip and above the mouth angles   disperse   et de la duplicité monstrueuse avec   planches coloriées de anditu et olfactu borough spinae praeparate cerea   cutaneous projection field   of all remote centers *icones oculi humani*   the point in the evening does not come out   but only in the morning   it drags   artificial rariora and its walls dilate and shrink   *matutinus*   need to think   alliance in stars   *organorum fabrica autem catoptrum microcosmicum de lactibus sive lacteis venis microcosmi in laminis aereis et ecce foramen unum in pariet liquido ostendens* the impulse of the winds to run   reveals this image   deep flaps of the reason a circle in a bigger circle vanish in plain view   word in suffused order   *in start*   there are tears in things   till it continues runn in this way its speed becomes normal   from an empty space in which we are awake

III.

(giorno#X)

il livello strada risplende   le schegge dell'asfalto sono bagnate di pioggia   infatti fuma splendente vapori iris
come quando emette con le labbra   un respiro   e sospirando si intensificano   le sofisticate luci delle griglie
di viaggio del segnale di velocità/modifica#   il ritrovo#   la funzione della vita tendenzia/sintesi#   in atmosfera
tutta contenuta attraverso   dietro luna   all'interno parato   un lembo del lenzuolo avanza dal letto   una sorta
di immagine fuori campo   un suono fuori campo   che passa dietro la testa e verticali distende   albedo inis
candor oris   dove il linguaggio si muoveva da solo

III.

(day#X)

the street level shines   the asphalt shards are wet with rain   in fact it smokes shiny vapors iris   as when it's emitted with lips   a breath   and sighing the sophisticated lights intensify the travel grids of the speed/change signall#   the gathering#   life function tendency/synthesis#   in the wholly contained atmosphere through   behind moon   inside wallpaper   a strip of the sheet advances from the bed   like an off-field image   an off-field sound   that passes behind the head   and extends verticals   *albedo inis candor oris* where language was moving by itself

CLAUDIO BERTONI

Claudio Bertoni (1946), poet, photographer, and visual artist, has published several books of poetry, photography, and translations, and has participated in numerous solo and group exhibitions, both in Chile and abroad. He has received a variety of distinctions as a poet and artist, such as the fellowship Corporación Amigos del Arte; a First Mention in the Municipal Prize of Poetry; the Guggenheim Scholarship for his work as a photographer and the poetry prize of the National Book and Reading Council. His poetic work is characterized by strong autobiographical remarks, the use of humor, the colloquial language, and the account of the quotidian. A certain kind of minimalism, linked to oriental philosophies, along with a permanent appeal to eroticism and desire, is also a feature of his work. During the sixties, along with Cecilia Vicuña and other artists, he founded the mythical group La Tribu No.

CARLOS SOTO ROMÁN

Carlos Soto Román (Valparaiso, 1977) is a pharmacist, poet and translator. He holds a Master of Bioethics from the University of Pennsylvania. He has published the following works in Chile and the United States: *La Marcha de los Quiltros* (1999), *Haikú Minero* (2007), *Cambio y Fuera* (2009), *Philadelphia's Notebooks* (Otoliths, 2011), *Chile Project: [Re-Classified]* (Gauss PDF, 2013), *The Exit Strategy* (Belladonna, 2014), and *Alternative Set of Procedures* (Corollary Press, 2014). As a translator, he has published *Do or DIY: Autoedición, Apropiación, Recontextualización y Plagio* (Das Kapital, 2013), *Bart* by Ron Silliman (Cuadro de Tiza, 2014), *coffee coffee* by Aram Saroyan (Libros del Pez Espiral, 2015), *Patriotismo* by Ryan Eckes (Libros del Pez Espiral, 2015), and *Por favor, no más poesía* by Derek Beaulieu (Libros del Pez Espiral, 2017). His work can be found in the following websites, magazines and journals: *Octopus, Otoliths, Fox Chase Review, Flying Fish, Revista Laboratorio, eL Paper, Caesura, Dear Navigator, Apiary, Eleven Eleven, Poetic Labor Project Blog, Where Eagles Dare, PEN American Center Blog, Gaceta de Estudios Latinoamericanos, Los Desconocidos de Siempre, Capitalism Nature Socialism, P-Queue, Summer Stock, Revista Grifo, COYDUP, Newport Review, Crux Desperationis, Letras en Línea, Hinchas de Poesía, Clock, The American Poetry Review, Mandorla, Jacket2,* and *Aufgabe.* He is a MacDowell Fellow and recipient of grants from the Chilean Council for Culture and the Arts for Creation and Translation projects. He also was the curator of the cooperative anthology of U.S. poetry *Elective Affinities.*

VIEJO

Eres
un segundo
más viejo

ESO SI QUE NO

Los hospitales no:

De mi dolor
a la tierra.

OLD

You are
one second
older

NO WAY

No hospitals:

From my pain
to the ground.

MARIA GRAZIA CALANDRONE

Maria Grazia Calandrone is a poet, playwright, performer, and writer based in Rome. She presents cultural programs on RAI Radio 3, contributes literary criticism to *Poesia*, *il manifesto* and *Corriere della Sera*, leads poetry workshops in schools, prisons, and mental health units, volunteers with the Piccoli Maestri kids' reading center, and directs the interview series *I volontari* for Corriere TV. Her books include: *Pietra di paragone* (Tracce, 1998 – Nuove Scrittrici Award), *La scimmia randagia* (Crocetti, 2003 – Pasolini Award), *Come per mezzo di una briglia ardente* (Atelier, 2005), *La macchina responsabile* (Crocetti, 2007), *Sulla bocca di tutti* (Crocetti, 2010 – Napoli, Sassari and Prata Awards), *Atto di vita nascente* (LietoColle, 2010), *La vita chiara* (transeuropa, 2011), *Serie fossile* (Crocetti, 2015 – Marazza and Tassoni Awards), *Gli Scomparsi – storie da "Chi l'ha visto?"* (Gialla Oro pordenonelegge, 2016 – Dessì Award), *Il bene morale* (Crocetti, 2017), the pseudo-novel *L'infinito mélo*, with an audio CD of her readings (Sossella Editions, 2011), and *Per voce sola*, a collection of dramatic monologues, drawings, and photos, with a CD by Sonia Bergamasco and EsTrio (ChiPiùNeArt, 2016). In 2017 she appeared in Donatella Baglivo's documentary *ll futuro in una poesia* and in Israeli filmmaker Omri Lior's *Poems With a View* project. Her poetry has been translated into over twenty languages.

JOHANNA BISHOP

Johanna Bishop grew up in Pennsylvania, was pigeonholed as a future translator by a standardized test in middle school, and has embraced that fate full-time since 2004. Her poetry translations include *Danza del ventre a Tel Aviv* by Karen Alkalay-Gut (co-translated into Italian with Andrea Sirotti, Kolibris, 2010) and *For the Maintenance of Landscape* by Mia Lecomte (with Brenda Porster, Guernica, 2012). Her translations of other contemporary poets have appeared in the anthology *Canone Inverso* (Gradiva, 2014) and in the reviews *TheFLR*, *Italian Poetry Review*, *Here—Notes from the Present*, and *Journal of Italian Translation*. She lives near Florence.

DA *SERIE FOSSILE* (CROCETTI, 2015)

© – fossile

metti una mano qui come una benda bianca, chiudimi gli occhi,
colma la soglia di benedizioni, dopo che
sei passata attraverso
l'oro verde dell'iride
come un'ape regale
e – pagliuzza
su pagliuzza,
d'oro e grano trebbiato –
hai fatto di me
il tuo favo di luce

una costellazione di api ruota sul tiglio
con saggezza inumana, un vorticare di intelligenze non si stacca
dall'albero del miele
            – sarebbe riduttivo dire amore
questa necessità della natura –
                        mentre un vuoto anteriore rimargina
tra fiore e fiore senza lasciare traccia:
                        usa la bocca, sfilami dal cuore
il pungiglione d'oro,
la memoria di un lampo che ha bruciato la mia forma umana
in una qualche preistoria

dove i pazzi accarezzano le pietre come fossero teste di bambini:
                        avvicinati, come la prima
tra le cose perdute
e quel volto si leva dalla pietra per sorridere ancora

24.5.13

Ϋ – albero, fossile

verrai nutrita
a lungo, avanti
nel tempo della vita, dai frutti
di un melo preistorico. in un futuro aprile, t'innalzerai
con la spina dorsale spinta
da una linfa nuova,

FROM *SERIE FOSSILE* (CROCETTI, 2015)

© – fossil

put one hand here like a white blindfold, close my eyes,
flood the threshold with blessings, after
passing through
the green gold of the iris
like a queenly bee
and – mote
by mote,
of gold and winnowed wheat –
turning me
into your hive of light

a bee constellation wheels around the linden
with inhuman wisdom, a gyration of minds sticking fast
to the honey tree
                – it would be reductive to call it love
this necessity of nature –
                   while a foregone emptiness heals over
without a trace between flower and flower:
                          use your mouth, ease the golden
stinger from my heart,
the memory of a flash of light that burnt my human form
in some prehistory

where madmen caress stones as if they were children's heads:
                          come closer, like the first
among lost things
and that face rises up from stone to smile again

5.24.13

Ϋ – tree, fossil

you will be fed
at length, further on
in the time of life, by the fruit
of a prehistoric apple tree. in a future April, you will rise up
with your spine spurred
by new sap,

ricorderai la dolcezza dell'albero che non voleva morire e ributtava e rifioriva, ogni volta
che lo tagliavi. girerai indietro
la testa, allungherai la mano, la bella mano che con tale dolcezza accarezzava
i rami aperti del melo
e mangerai. allora tornerò nella tua bocca con la leggerezza della luce. e ancora,
al calor bianco del nostro tempo estivo, mangerai
la mela che ha pescato
al fondo del tempo, il frutto rosso e gonfio
come un'arteria, che scorre
dalla mia vita alla tua vita,
ma lontano, ma sotto, là dove non arriva la ragione,
nei luoghi inarrestabili. dimentica
l'albero. non pensare più a niente, soffiami via. che resti solo vita per la tua vita,

24.8.14

♈— insieme MRK 1034

le spirali delle due ammoniti sul tuo petto
ripetono la forma delle galassie gemelle
PGC 9074 e PGC 9071
della costellazione del Triangolo

una (la 9074, di tipo Sa) mostra una sporgenza luminosa, l'intenzione di un'alba, ma porta i bracci avvolti
strettamente intorno al proprio nucleo

l'altra, la galassia che si srotola più a Nord nel nero siderale (la 9071, di tipo Sb), ha allargato le braccia da un
discreto numero di anni-luce.
il buio dell'universo è sottoposto a magnetismi incommensurabili. altrimenti, è cieco.
questa forma di abbraccio
disabitata, questa custode con le ali aperte nel silenzio profondo, reca un dolore alla spalla destra. è un oggetto
celeste dai tendini infiammati, a Nord-Est del tuo cielo

le due galassie sono scientificamente inseparabili. cito, da un articolo di Eleonora Ferroni, in Notiziario
dell'Istituto Nazionale di AstroFisica: "sono abbastanza vicine da sentire l'una la gravità dell'altra, ma non ci
sono disturbi gravitazionali visibili"

entrambe hanno prodotto "giovani e calde stelle retrostanti", mentre "formazioni stellari più antiche e fredde"
pulsano, gialle del giallo bestiale della savana, accanto al loro nucleo
e un corteo di stelle ormai lontane le circonda, come una corona di detriti

le due astrali Signore delle porte accanto hanno lasciato scie di sangue e dolcezza, scorie di amori ormai
assorbite dal rombo dei venti galattici. ma la forza di gravità di ciascuna nei confronti dell'altra le porterà a
confondersi in un unico grande fenomeno, in un abbraccio pieno.

you will remember the sweetness of the tree that would not die and resprouted and reblossomed, every time
you cut it. you will turn
back, stretch out your hand, the lovely hand that so sweetly caressed
the open branches of the apple tree
and you will eat. then I will come back into your mouth gently as light. and again,
in the white heat of our summer time, you will eat
the apple you fished
out of the depths of time, the fruit red and swollen
as an artery, running
from my life to your life,
but far away, underneath, where reason doesn't reach,
in the unstoppable places. forget
the tree. turn off your thoughts, waft me away. let there remain only life for your life,

8.24.14

Union of MRK 1034

the spirals of the two ammonites on your chest
echo the shape of the twin galaxies
PGC 9074 and PGC 9071
in the constellation of the Triangle

one of them (9074, type Sa) shows a bright protrusion, the inkling of a dawn, but has its arms tightly
wrapped around its own nucleus

the other, the galaxy that unfurls to the north in the sidereal dark (9071, type Sb) has stretched its arms more
than a few light-years out.
the black space of the universe is moved by incommensurable magnetisms. otherwise, it's blind.
this sort of uninhabited
embrace, this guardian opening its wings in the deep silence, bears an ache in its right shoulder. a celestial
object with inflamed tendons, in your northeastern sky

the two galaxies are scientifically inseparable. I quote, from an article by Eleonora Ferroni, in the newsletter
of the National Institute of Astrophysics: "they are close enough to feel each other's gravity, but there are no
visible gravitational disturbances"

both have produced "young, hot stars lying behind," while "older, cooler star formations" pulse, gold like the
feral gold of the savanna, close to their nucleus
and a chorus of receding stars surrounds them, like a coronet of debris

the two astral neighbor ladies have left trails of blood and sweetness, the dross of lives long absorbed by the
thundering of galactic winds. but the gravitational pull of each to the other will lead them to converge into a
single great phenomenon, into a full embrace.

l'articolo chiude infatti così: "tra qualche centinaio di milioni di anni le due strutture si fonderanno, perché l'attrazione gravitazionale che già le vincola avrà definitivamente attirato le due ormai inseparabili gemelle".

sacre stelle pazienti. oggetti che non forzate
la curvatura spaziotemporale, limpide forze che state
nell'intervallo naturale
che sulla terra viene detto rispetto.
le stelle hanno la calma delle stelle.

questa forma cretacica fossile ha un disegno terrestre: le sue spirali, formate da rigoni d'inchiostro organico, riproducono la rotazione delle due galassie. cose forse avvenute nello stesso momento in terra e in cielo. 180 milioni di anni fa. cose delle quali siamo il futuro. o l'utopia.
questa insiemistica fantascientifica, lo stadio fossile-astrale della materia, è il mio dono per te.

in attesa di formare l'insieme al quale sono destinate, le due vicine svolgono un'intensa attività interiore, che porta entrambe a uno sprigionamento di energie attive, utili alla creazione di pianeti. esse sono due splendide officine, due fervidi laboratori di stelle. esse irradiano luce.

l'osservatorio on-line del telescopio spaziale Hubble della NASA-ESA, che le ha individuate, ha pubblicato la notizia il 24.6.2013 (di quel pomeriggio, ricordo un allegrissimo braccio di ferro al bar, sotto una parete di grappoli di glicine. non ha vinto nessuno. le nostre forze sono strutture equivalenti e complesse)

la suggestiva scoperta ha subito rimbalzato sui siti astronomici internazionali, nei primi giorni del luglio 2013. di quei giorni ricordo un dialogo sull'ironia della natura: scoprivamo che gli alveoli polmonari e il meconio si formano nel medesimo stadio evolutivo del feto umano: pneuma e feci. come sempre. l'umano.

poi, ricordo la musica di un amore immortale sulla rovina di Massenzio: "e si 'na stella canta pe' ammore rimmane 'n cielo mill'anne e nun more". poi, ricordo un sorriso, così profondo da perdonare i morti, invincibile come la forza gravitazionale che sulla terra viene detta destino. e poi ricordo un suono di campane, semplice come il caldo della tua bocca

che dura qui, ben oltre la mia vita

16.11.14

the article closes saying: "in several hundred million years the two structures will merge, since the gravitational attraction that already binds them will have definitively drawn together the already inseparable twins."

patient holy stars. objects that do not force
the spacetime curve, limpid forces that remain
in the natural interval
that on earth is called respect.
the stars have the calm of stars.

this Cretaceous fossil form has an earthly design: its spirals, formed by thick strokes of organic ink, depict the rotation of the two galaxies. things that perhaps took place on the same time in earth and in heaven. 180 million years ago. things of which we are the future. or the utopia.
this science-fiction union of set theory, the fossil/astral stage of matter, is my gift to you.

waiting to form the union to which they are destined, the two neighbors carry out intense inner activities which lead both to give off active energy, useful for creating planets. they are two splendid foundries, two feverish mills of stars. they radiate light.

the online observatory of the NASA/ESA Hubble Space Telescope, which identified them, published the news on 06.24.2013 (from that afternoon, I recall a gleeful arm-wrestling match at the café, under a wall of wisteria blossoms. nobody won. our forces are equivalent and complex structures)

the evocative discovery instantly spread through international astronomy sites, in the early days of July 2013. From those days I remember a dialogue about the irony of nature: we discovered that the alveoli in the lungs and meconium in the gut form at the same evolutionary stage of the human fetus: pneuma and feces. as always. humanity.

then, I remember a song of immortal love on the ruins of the Basilica Maxentius: "e si 'na stella canta pe' ammore rimmane 'n cielo mill'anne e nun more". then, I remember a smile, deep enough to absolve the dead, invincible as the gravitational force that on earth is called destiny. and then I remember a ringing of bells, simple as the warmth of your mouth

that lingers on here, well beyond my life

11.16.14

MARINA YUSZCZUK

Marina Yuszczuk is a poet who received her PhD in literature. She works as a journalist and a film critic for the cultural supplement *Las12* of *Página 12* and for the magazine *La Agenda*. She has published various books of poetry: *Lo que la gente hace* (Blatt & Ríos, 2012), *Madre soltera* (Mansalva, 2013), and *La ola de frío polar* (Gog y Magog, 2015). With the press Rosa Iceberg, which she founded with Tamara Tenenbaum and Emilia Erbetta, she recently published *Los arreglos* (2017), her first book of prose. Her first novel, *La inocencia,* was recently published by Iván Rosado.

ALEXIS ALMEIDA

Alexis Almeida grew up in Chicago. Her recent poems and translations have appeared or are forthcoming in *BOMB*, *The Brooklyn Rail*, *Folder*, *Quarterly West*, *Prelude*, *Dusie*, *Action Yes*, and elsewhere. She is an assistant editor at *Asymptote* and a contributing editor at *The Elephants*. Her chapbook of poems, *Half-Shine*, is recently out from Dancing Girl Press, and her translation of Florencia Castellano's *Propiedades vigiladas [Monitored Properties]* is recently out from Ugly Duckling Presse. Her translation of Roberta Iannamico's *Tendal [Wreckage]* is recently out from Toad Press. She was a Fulbright research fellow to Argentina, and is currently compiling and co-translating an anthology of contemporary female poets living in Argentina. She lives in Providence where she teaches writing.

18

Mmm, no. La verdad...
Ayer escribí ese poema objetivista donde decía que tal vez nos separemos pero yo
no estaba en el poema, o algo así
o estaba oculta en el orden de sus versos
a veces hago eso.
El poeta que escribe sus versos con una dicción, digamos
tan meditada
no está flotando en la tormenta
de la experiencia
en el volcán de la experiencia, porque la experencia
es un volcán
y la poesía...
debe ser una piedra.

20

      En una película que me gustó, un alpinista que estaba por batir un record contaba que cuando se escala una pared de una montaña, frente a la pared, no se piensa. Después dijo – con ojos de celeste glaciar y una sonrisa algo loca que mostraba demasiado los dientes, enormes como bloques de hielo – que cuando miraba esas paredes en las montañas sentía que eran pizarras gigantes en las que podía dibujar líneas. Eso es escalar, desde acá hasta acá, y otra allá, y otra allá, recorridos que antes no existían, líneas que nadie más podría ver y que van a quedar para siempre marcadas, algo así.

      Y nosotros, ¿qué estamos haciendo?

35

Pero, pero, pero...
esto y lo otro,
esto y aquello más,
o quizás lo primero

las ideas extendidas como sábanas y arrugadas
como sábanas que no se cambian muy seguido,
un estado de contradicción tan plena.

18

Mmm, no. The truth is...
Yesterday I wrote this "objectivist" poem where I said that maybe we would separate
but I wasn't in the poem, or something like that
or I was hidden in the ordering of the lines
sometimes I do that.
The poet that writes her lines with diction, so to speak,
that is so thought-out
isn't floating in the storm
of experience
in the flood of experience, because experience is a flood
and poetry
should be a rock.

20

      In a movie that I like, a mountain-climber who was about to beat a record tells of how when you climb
the side of a mountain, faced with this side, you don't think. Afterwards he said – with glacial blue eyes and
something of a crazy smile that showed too much teeth, giant blocks of ice – that when he looked at the sides .
of the mountains he felt they were giant chalkboards on which you could draw lines. That is climbing, from
here to here, and then from there, and then there, paths that didn't exist before, lines that no one else could see
and that will always be there drawn in, something like that.

      And us, what are we doing?

35

But, but, but...
this and the other
this and that other thing
or maybe the first thing

longwinded ideas like sheets that are wrinkled
like sheets that aren't changed very often,
a state of such plain contradiction.

GIANCARLO HUAPAYA

Giancarlo Huapaya (Lima, Peru) is author of the books *Estado y Contemplación/Canción de Canción se Gana*, *Polisexual*, and *Taller Sub Verso*, and the editor of the anthology *Pulenta Pool: Peruvian Poets in the United States* (Hostos Review, 2017). As a curator of visual poetry, he has presented exhibitions at the Mission Cultural Center For Latino Arts in San Francisco, and at the University of Arizona Poetry Center in Tucson. Previously, he was the advisor of the editorial and music industry policies of Cultural Industries in Lima, and he was the director of the Lima Poetry Festival during its first three years. He also is Founder and Editor of Cardboard House Press, a nonprofit publishing house for Latin American and Spanish literature in translation. His poems and translations have appeared in *Transtierros* (LAT), *Vallejo & Co* (Peru), *Poesía* (Venezuela), *Zunái* (Brazil), *Jacket 2* (US), and *Anomaly* (US), among others.

ILANA LUNA

Ilana Luna holds a Ph.D. in Hispanic Languages and Literature from the University of California, Santa Barbara, with an additional emphasis in literary translation. She is an Assistant professor of Latin American Studies at Arizona State University where she teaches on film, literature, and cultural studies. Luna is the author of *Adapting Gender: Mexican Feminisms from Literature to Film* (SUNY Press) that considers the subversive potential of film adaptation of literary texts that intersect with feminist discourses in a neoliberal Mexico. She is a board member of Cardboard House Press, a founding member of the feminist collective entre nosOtr@s in Phoenix, Arizona, and has served on the board of the Arizona Interfaith Alliance for Worker Justice.

taller sub verso

H

Si desean pincharse, pinchar a otrx, o que los pinchen, el día será perfecto para infectarse de duración. Hiperactuarán con el ojo cubierto de papel mojado rojo en forma de corazón,

disritmia

cuando ingieren la de fresa, la de chocolate y la de vainilla por un mismo ojo.

Lo sonoro variará entre un ruido promiscuo y uno de plasma,

el vj los mezclará con adelanto de oráculo.

Los cabellos se mutilan.

Los cañones multimedia operarán nuestra apariencia cada vez que *la belleza se monte en nuestras piernas.*

Eco. Se performatiza la calvicie y descuida fidelidad. Como un noise para *detener el tiempo.*

Este eco se reiterará por más tiempo de lo detenido. Lo detenido será sustraído. *La poética del espacio* se pincha. Pinchazos libres de jurisdicción. Eco. Adicción libre de censura. Dicción suena, ambulan los conciertos.

Implosión de *ruido stars* en la *memoria episódica.* Eco

Dé vuelta al vocablo que pronuncia como proxeneta.

El mecanismo de poleas dibuja en bocas los vocablos sobresalientes de este papel auditivo, se exponen en el mutismo de tu grafía deshecha. Descifra códigos con sangrados en cada exhalación de la letra.

Eco aché.

La heroína del alquitrán negro y el indígena guaraní graban el dolor de sus registros en un disco de nogal e ishpingo. Continuos pedazos de enzimas surcan los oxígenos, a veces como resultado de mezcla

imitan avispadas serpentinas acarameladas o se pudren como ansiosas flores púrpuras

en el flujo tridimensional de este *papel* papiloma.

Nos sentimos la vida secreta del decibel diptongo

Den bellotas,

sub verse workshop

H

If you want to inject yourself, inject someone else, or have them inject you, the day will be perfect for a long-term infection. You will hyperact with an eye covered by a red, wet heart-shaped piece of paper

dysrhythmia

when you ingest strawberry, chocolate, and vanilla through the same eye

Sound will modulate between a promiscuous noise and a plasmic one,

the vj will spin them with the prescience of an oracle.

Strands of hair mutilate themselves.

The multimedia cannons will manipulate our appearance each time that *beauty climbs up our legs*

Echo. Baldness is performatized and fidelity overlooked. Like a noise to *stop time.*

This echo will reverberate for more time than is stopped. Everything stopped will be expelled. *The poetics of space* is injected. Injections free from jurisdiction. Echo. Addiction free from censorship. Diction sounds, concerts deambulate.

Implosion of *noise stars* in the *episodic memory.* Echo

Reverse the term that pronounces like a procurer.

The pulley mechanism draws the keynote terms of this audio paper in mouths, you are exposed in the mutism of your broken writing. Decipher the codes with bleeds in each exhalation of a letter.

Echo aché.

Black tar heroine and the native Guaraní engrave the pain of their records on a walnut and ishpingo disk. Continuous pieces of enzymes plow through the oxygen, sometimes as the result of the mixing

they imitate sharp, caramelized streamers or they rot like anxious purple flowers

in the tridimensional flux of this *paper* papilloma.

We feel like the secret life of the diphthong decibel

Give acorns,

que imaginen aspectos de sinestesia y exploren la decorativa del desmayo con ecos hipnóticos. Brillan cristales en las orillas que delatan las fosas de sus fogosidades, irrumpan la mirada estática con enceguecedores sones de vapores de despedida.

Eco mudo recuerda.

No, ustedes son verduras listas para el rayador

Suena tu cuerpecito contra la rejilla del metal. Sienten la multitud de daños adolescentes.

J

Este taller será sumergido en el mar. Ahí vamos a construir una ciudad erógena, con medusas y malaguas rodeadas por corales sicodélicos, la simbiosis rejuvenece con revoluciones de sales de todas partes del torbellino. Suena la vida del cardumen, bailamos rojos como pulpos.

Este taller ahora será enterrado en el subsuelo. Antibiótico y sísmico. En las profundidades sembraremos nuestros adeenes para que la luna fecunde genomas, en mitosis expresarán seres dendrofílicxs que invadirán el futuro. Sus dominios tendrán que sobrepasar las vidas y las muertes. Se transborda y se monta incluso, lo intangible y lo abstracto.

Barajen el carnaval de climas y usen sus máscaras.

Podrás ser un fanzine panfletario

que transita por lo electrónico

o un batracio nasal contracultural que suspira terror

o una evolución criadora y programática de grados farenheits

o una manía errante de viento de nubes metálicas

o un exorcismo mordaz para números de letras zombis

o la significancia de la octava parte del organismo negro de esta composición

o los vicios mudos del ribete y la línea onda girante

o los versus que ideologizan las espinas desde tus recibos de servicios

o lo necio de andar con los tobillos cortados emplumando ángeles ninfómanas

that imagine aspects of synesthesia and explore the decorations of swooning with hypnotic echoes. Crystals sparkle at the edges revealing the graves of their passions, they burst through the static gaze with blinding sounds of departing vapors.

Mute echo remembers.

No, you all are vegetables ready for the grater

Your little body bangs against the metal grating. Feel the multitude of adolescent damages.

J

This workshop will be submerged in the sea. There we will construct an erogenous city, with jellyfish and man-of-war surrounded by psychedelic coral, the symbiosis rejuvenates with salt revolutions from every part of the vortex. The life of the school vibrates, we dance red like octopuses.

The workshop will now be buried underground. Antibiotic and seismic. In the depths we will sow our DNAs so that the moon can fertilize genomes, in mitosis they will express dendrophiliac beings that will invade the future. Their dominion will have to surpass life and death. It transfers and even overlays the intangible with the abstract.

Mix up the carnival of climates and use your masks.

You can be a propagandistic fanzine

that travels electronically

or a nasal counter-culture toad that exhales terror

or a breeding and programmatic evolution in degrees farenheit

or an errant mania of metal-cloud wind

or a mordent exorcism for zombie-letter numbers

or the significance of an eigth of the black organism of this composition

or the mute vices of the edging and the gyrating wavy line

or the oppositions that ideologize the thorns in your service bills

or the foolishness of walking with ankles cut and feathered with nymphomaniac angels

o el entusiasmo de primerizo imán sonador de cartones
o el diletante alfabeto que pretende decidir competencias

o la orden que hostiga nuestro picado cooperativo

o los garabatos de espíritu en mayólicas honguiviejas en baños universitarios

o la continuación de grabaciones de referentes a(ni)mados.

O

Muestra de holopoesía. Método gonzo, inestabilidades tridimensionales.

Vueltas luminosas alrededor de la avalancha. La contaminación de soportes suma lucidez, detalla letrismo, la fónica aleatoria ventila sus corrupciones de pensamiento, rotan bruscos los meteoritos, las lenguas serpentean los hincapiés. Se abrazan furiosas las sedas cenizas, en ellas un tenso rostro tras un hocico rupestre tras una respiración tupida pinta los ciclos de las siluetas de los niños elásticos que irritan el espejo.

Hambriento de vidrio, ranura que se mueve, sus texturas son traducidas en psicodélicas polillas, colmillos de fuego, píldoras rosas, membranas sobre laberintos de sensores bimetales de amores furtivos, perfumes performances, esgrima al compás de galanteos, cabezas de pollos recitan músculos, caen estalactitas, explotan ataúdes con pica pica.

Revolución universal de bacterias.

Adictas al autoexamen, la autoironía, el atentado.

En cualquier lugar de cualquier momento desprenderemos nuestras bombas contra la dictadura de lo normal, desprenderemos amor aterrorizante. El tren de cuerpos algodonados y dulces es vidrioso y ardiente. Su reproducción se imprimirá con destellos insurgentes.

or the enthusiasm of a brand new magnetic soundbox
or the literate diletant that aspires to judging competitions

or the order that harasses our cooperative banging

or the spirit scribbles on old fungusy tiles in university bathrooms

or the sequel to recordings of lovely/lively examples

O

Sample of holopoetry. Gonzo method, tridimensional instabilities.

Luminous laps around the avalanche. The contamination of foundations enhances lucidity, it describes Lettrism in detail, the random sound-bytes ventilate their corruptions of thought, the meteorites rotate abruptly, tongues snake around the emphases. The ashy silks furiously embrace, in them, a tense countenance behind a rock snout after a thick breath, paints the cycles of silhouettes of elastic children that irritate the mirror.

Hungry for glass, the opening moves, its textures are translated into psychedelic moths, fangs of fire, pink pills, membranes over labyrinths of bimetal sensors of furtive loves, perfume performances, fencing to the beat of courtships, chicken heads recite muscles, stalactites fall, coffins explode with confetti.

A universal revolution of bacteria.

Addicts of self-examination, self-deprecation, the attack.

In any place at any moment we will release our bombs against the dictatorship of normalcy, we will unleash terrorizing love. The train of cotton candy bodies is made of glass and fire. Its reproduction will print out with insurgent flashes.

ANDREA INGLESE

Andrea Inglese (Italy, 1967) is a poet, essayist, novelist, blogger, translator, and literary activist that lives in Paris. He has a PhD in Comparative Literature and has held teaching positions in Contemporary Italian Literature at the University of Paris III. In 2003, he wrote an essay on the theory of the novel, "L'eroe segreto [The secret hero]." Other literary essays on the novel and poetry are included in a number of volumes in Italy and France. He has published eight books of poetry and prose. One of his most recent poetry books, *Lettere alla Reinserzione Culturale del Disoccupato* [*Letters to the Cultural Rehabilitation of the Unemployed*] has appeared in an Italian (Italic Pequod, 2013), French (translated in French by Stéphane Bouquet, NOUS, 2013) and English edition (translated in English by Sara Elena Rossetti, Patrician Press, 2017). His anthology of the French poet Jean-Jacques Viton, *Il commento definitivo: Poesie 1984-2008*, was published by Metauro in 2009. His first novel, *Parigi è un desiderio* [*Paris is a desire*], was published by Ponte alle Grazie in 2016. He is a member of the literary blog *Nazione Indiana* (www.nazioneindiana.com). He is on the editorial committee of "alfabeta2" (www.alfabeta2.it). He is the curator of Descrizione del mondo [Description of the World], a collective project based on exhibitions and on a website (www.descrizionedelmondo.it).

SARA ELENA ROSSETTI

Sara Elena Rossetti was born in 1980 and lives near Milan. She teaches English and translates work from English into Italian. She has collaborated on translations of poems by Christina Georgina Rossetti, including "Goblin Market" ("Il mercato dei folletti," Edizioni San Marco dei Giustiniani, 2009) and "The Prince's Progress" ("Il cammino del principe," Galassia Arte, 2014). She has worked on subtitling for art documentaries, include *Travelling into Fluxus* (Irene Di Maggio, 2014), and directed a short documentary based on interviews about dreams (Favola di Mattoni, 2009). She has published some illustrated books using letter press printing (Edizioni Pulcinoelefante) and her first poetry collection is *Arcobaleno-Rainbow* (Patrician Press, 2014). Her last translation is *Letters to the Cultural Rehabilitation of the Unemployed* by Andrea Inglese, that has just been published by Patrician Press.

DA LE CIRCOSTANZE DELLA FRASE,
IN *LETTERE ALLA REINSERZIONE CULTURALE DEL DISOCCUPATO*

NON STA SUCCEDENDO PIÙ NIENTE, non succede niente, non è mai successo niente, da miliardi di anni non succede, nella mia testa assolutamente niente, non potrà mai succedere, che sia dentro o fuori la mia testa, che sia sulla mia testa, come corona di polline, nube, monito immane, oppure intorno, sotto la mia testa, tra i piedi, come rametto, addome di vespa, tappo graffiato, neppure sotto i piedi succede niente, ancora niente, negli ossari, nella falde, nel buio minerale, per un sacco di tempo non succederà niente, niente di cui si possa dire è successo, è successa una cosa, una stupidissima cosa, un b, un b piccolo, anche la metà, anche niente, per errore, fosse pure per errore non succederà mai, nei giornali, ogni giorno, lo ammettono, dentro e fuori le righe, nei laboratori lo confermano, nel mezzo del massacro, se ti chini su quello, proprio riverso, affumicato in faccia, a cui stai per cavare il cuore, lui pure te lo sibila, nonostante la nostra professionale distruzione, dice, neanche sotto le bombe, nelle macerie, accade molto più di niente.

NON CI PENSO PER ORA ALLA FINE DEL MONDO, non ne parlerò adesso, non subito, che comunque avverrà, anzi avviene, ma remotissima, con schianti violenti su certi fondali, o il millimetro, quel millimetro di più o di meno, d'acqua, uranio, o ghiaccio, anidride, o qualsiasi cosa, che cambia tutto, azzera infallibilmente il bosco, polverizza il sistema nervoso, annienta occhi, ali, larve, o come il godimento della luce, se venisse meno il godimento della luce, di quando entra di traverso, a ondate ininterrotte, la mattina, anche dalla finestra quadrata e piccola del bagno, se mancasse quella reazione animale, o semplicemente di foglia, quel transito vegetale al calore, ma non ci penso, per ora, all'epidemia, alla glottide che gonfia, al perimetro che smaglia dell'iride, guardo i tuoi piedi nudi, in cucina, con enorme meraviglia, mentre fissano e placano il pavimento, mentre tengono divaricato lo spazio, ancora percorribile, per qualche attimo, prima dei nuovi, ultimi crolli.

CERTO CHE TI VEDO E TU MI PARLI, e che sai ridere, e non so davvero come, fino a dove riesci a ridere, e a parlare, e penso anche che con uno sforzo continuo, fatto subito, afferrandomi ai bordi del tavolo, posso sorridere anch'io, posso con naturalezza ricambiarti un sorriso, è solo che me lo devo costruire, e bisogna essere cauti a formarlo, se sbaglio la piega, viene fuori magari qualcosa di buio e mostruoso, o magari delle lacrime, e proprio agli angoli degli occhi, mentre tu volevi solo ridere, anzi ci riuscivi, quasi avessi un meccanismo interno, o solo acquistato una macchina, e di continuo la azionassi, una resistente macchina di denti, tale da prolungare sorrisi per giorni, e io invece privo di artifici, con le mie sole forze, pescando dove possibile un riflesso, un tremito, che agisca sulle labbra mie, senza sfigurarle soprattutto, e poi ascoltarti, che se riuscissi almeno ad ascoltarti, ma dentro questo attutimento, come posato in fondo al sommergibile, tutto assordato dai piccoli rumori della mia disperazione, è difficile capire le singole parole, o ricordarsi di come fanno assieme una frase, quella che mi stai dicendo, ma da tutti questi schianti, che mi rendono così sordo e disperato, potrei trarre una tremenda forza, come una gioia, e rovesciare molte risate, a sapere invertire, commutare, questo lavorio, questi rumori di ogni punto, di ogni istante.

FROM CIRCUMSTANCES OF THE SENTENCE, FOUND IN *LETTERS TO THE CULTURAL REHABILITATION OF THE UNEMPLOYED*

NOTHING IS HAPPENING, nothing happens, nothing has ever happened, for billions of years nothing has happened, in my head absolutely nothing, nothing will happen inside or outside my head, on my head, like a pollen crown, cloud, a dreadful warning, or around, under my head, between my feet, like a small branch, wasp abdomen, scratched cork, not even under my feet, nothing happens, still nothing in the ossuary, in the groundwater, in the mineral dark, for a long time nothing will happen, nothing what you can say has happened, something happened, a stupid small thing happened, a b, a small b, even a half of it, or nothing by mistake, even if only by mistake, it will never happen, they say it in newspapers every day, inside and outside the lines, they confirm it in labs, when you are in the middle of a massacre, if you bend on the one whose heart you are going to pull out, his body laying prone, his blackened face, he also hisses it to you, besides our professional destruction, he says, not even under bombs, beneath the rubble, more than nothing happens.

I'M NOT THINKING NOW OF THE END OF THE WORLD, I won't talk about it now, not right now, but the end will happen, well it is happening, but so very far away, with violent crashes over some seabeds, or the millimetre, that millimetre more or less, of water, uranium, ice, anhydride or something else, changing everything, unfailingly eliminating the woods, crushing the nervous system, wiping out eyes, wings, grubs, or like enjoying light, if enjoying light were less, when it enters at an angle, in the morning, in never-ending waves even from the little square bathroom window, if that animal reaction were missing, or that simple leaf one, that vegetal transit to heat, but I don't think about it now, I don't think about the epidemic, the swelling glottis, the cut at the edge of the iris, I look at your naked feet, in the kitchen, with enormous wonder, while they are fixed and calm the floor, while they keep the space open wide, still accessible, for some moments, before the last, new collapse.

OF COURSE I SEE YOU AND YOU TALK TO ME, you can laugh, and I don't know how, up to what point you can laugh, and talk, and I also think that trying through continuous effort, immediate, grasping the edges of a table, I can laugh too, spontaneously smiling at you, it is just that I have to fabricate that smile, and one should be careful in forming it, if I make a mistake in the crease, maybe something dark and monstrous could come out, or maybe some tears, right at the corners of the eyes, but you just wanted to laugh, indeed you can do it, as if you had an internal mechanism, or just bought a machine, and you were continuously switching this machine on, a machine of teeth, resistant, able to extend smiles for days, instead I am deprived of any artifices, with only my efforts, catching a reflection where possible, a tremor on my lips, most of all without defacing them, and then listening to you, if I were at least able to listen to you, but inside this deadening, lying at the bottom of the submarine, deafened by the small noises of my desperation, it's difficult to understand single words, or how together they form a sentence, the one you are saying to me, but I could gain great strength from all these pangs making me desperate and deaf, like a delight, and overturn many laughs, if I were able to invert, commute, all this intense activity, these noises from everywhere, every moment.

Made in the USA
Columbia, SC
23 January 2023

10498764R10061